GW01465265

CATCHING FIRE

EDWIN ROBERTSON

eagle

Guildford, Surrey

Copyright © 1993 Edwin Robertson

British Library Cataloguing-in-Publication Data. A catalogue record for
this book is available from the British Library.

Published by Eagle, an imprint of Inter Publishing Service (IPS) Ltd,
59 Woodbridge Road, Guildford, Surrey GU1 4RF.

All Scripture quotations, unless otherwise noted, are taken from the *Holy
Bible, Revised Standard Bible*.

Typeset by The Electronic Book Factory, Fife.
Printed in the UK by HarperCollins Manufacturing, Glasgow.

ISBN No: 0 86347 105 6

CONTENTS

PREFACE

Enthusiasm in the eighteenth Century was a word which, in religious circles, provoked mixed feelings. Understood, however, in its more general sense it was always welcomed as an opportunity for the fire of God's love in the Gospel of Jesus Christ once again to be proclaimed vibrantly in the world. It was in that sense that John Wesley, inspired by the love of God, brought renewal and grace when his 'heart was strangely warmed'.

Edwin Robertson shows us in this impressionistic review of the Focolare Movement how Chiara Lubich and those who have followed her have contributed similarly to the rebirth of Christ's church in the twentieth century. It could be argued that the continued vitality of Christian discipleship and of the church itself has been due to a series of revolutions throughout the centuries. In the thirteenth century Francis, once again with the fire of God's love, was able to bring a new life and commitment to God's church. It was a rebirth that has never been lost. As one reads through these pages one reflects upon the similarity between that medieval revolution and the power of the Focolare to bring new life in so many ways.

That new life has been imparted to the church not only in different parts of the world, but in different aspects of our understanding of the Gospel and its meaning for our daily life. Chiara Lubich talks about 'the world always moving towards unity'. The implications of such a truth still remain to be taken seriously by most of us throughout God's church. It is also clear from Edwin Robertson's work that Chiara's movement has wrought a revolution in the understanding of the role of women in the Roman Catholic Church. Remaining loyal to the hierarchy and to Catholic teaching, a new life has been breathed into this area. Similar reflection could be made about the Focolare Movement and our understanding of the Eucharist.

As we read these pages we realise that the heart of the Focolare Movement will always lie in Italy. For Italy is the home of Chiara and it is the wellspring of the enthusiasm and rebirth of God's love which Focolare has exemplified throughout its history. Nevertheless, paradoxically, the book begins in Britain, indeed in London. It gathers together an assorted group of people, Anglicans and Roman Catholics, and it shows how far the influence of Focolare has permeated into God's church throughout the world. My hope is that many people will read this book and be inspired and enthused by the vision of the 'warm hearth' which is described in the name Focolare itself. Such an inspiration will help the family of nations to be offered an example in the family that God had given in his church.

Once again, as in his other writings, God's church owes a debt of great gratitude to Edwin Robertson for his clarity of expression, his authentic love of the Gospel and the breadth of his sympathies, which have allowed him to contribute so much throughout his long and active Christian life.

George Cantuar
Lambeth Palace
February 1993

CATCHING FIRE

CHAPTER ONE
MEET THE FOCOLARE

In a long winding street in West London with moderately large semi-detached houses, there is one which looks much like all the others. If there is anything that makes it stand out, it is that it is very well kept and its lights are welcoming; but the main difference is the kind of life lived by the people in that house. There are six of them, all men in their thirties or forties, who constitute a family. They use an Italian word, *'focolare'* to describe themselves, but that simply means 'hearth' or 'fireplace' and only emphasizes that they are a family. They all work and they share their incomes. As they have responsible and fairly senior posts – an accountant, a consultant in information technology, teachers, a supervisor of teaching, a publisher – they have adequate incomes. They live carefully, not extravagantly and therefore have money to spare. As they belong to an international movement they make that money available so that less fortunate focolares may also have a reasonable standard of living; and as the movement is engaged in a great deal of social and educational work, so some of the money goes to that. As far as they can, both domestically in their own 'Focolare' and throughout the movement, they follow the pattern of the Church described in the Acts of the Apostles:

'Now the company of those who believed were of one heart and soul, and no one said that any of the things which he possessed was his own, but they had everything in common'. (Acts 4:32)

This sharing does not seem to make them feel restricted. The focolare in West London is a very happy and sociable group of men, and an evening with them is enjoyable, for they are 'given to hospitality'.

Of the six who live in the house at present, three are Roman Catholic and three are Anglican. They worship in different churches and are all regular at Mass or Holy Communion. They find no conflict in their different denominations and have a common spirituality, held together by the movement and in their daily meditations. Those daily meditations are often held separately during working days, but together at weekends. The movement has a good selection of devotional literature and a discipline of a biblical text each month. The text which is called a 'Word of Life' is chosen by the founder of the movement, Chiara Lubich, in consultation with its leadership. It is the same throughout the world. A commentary is provided and all members of the movement consciously try to live that text during the month. They feel the New Testament is too much when taken as a whole, whereas a verse at a time is manageable. That kind of common sense logic goes through the whole movement.

The Focolare in West London

These six men are normal people in middle life, devoted and committed to their churches and striving to live what they call 'the Ideal', which is God. As Chiara Lubich, the founder, said to her father when he asked, 'What is this Ideal that you talk about?' 'It is love, Father, it is love.' One of its principal characteristics is 'Unity'. These six men discuss everything and come to a common mind before they take action. This does not mean that they always agree, but they always listen and understand the reasons for any differences. For example they discuss politics and may well vote differently, but they respect one another's decision. Who are they?

The senior member is Tim, 42 years old, Catholic, and a specialist in information technology. He worked for some years with British Gas and is now a consultant to them. Being a consultant gives him more time to devote to the movement and he looks after members in different parts of the South of England. The movement has a very big children's work and he has a special interest in children of 9 to 13 years old. Tim is from Liverpool and has earned his seniority in this focolare by long service. He has been a member for eighteen years!

Bartolemeo, called Tomeo, is one of the most recent members. He had just arrived when I went to see them and is a much travelled member of the movement. He is a Catalonian from Majorca, and has done many different jobs – insurance representative, dealing with accident claims; a teacher in Barcelona; a gardener in Switzerland; an agriculturist in Madrid; on the Argentinian Embassy staff in Rawalpindi, Pakistan. He learnt English in Switzerland and in England and is now a very lively member of the family. He is the same age as Tim. He arrived from Grottaferrata, near Rome, where he was studying English again. He is well equipped to teach, or to garden – or to do almost anything.

Carlo, who is not much younger, is an Italian from that part of Italy which used to be called, 'the red triangle', because of its communist support. He is the accountant both professionally and for the family. He has been a member of this focolare since 1983.

The other three, Mark, Callan, and Mike are all English, ranging in age from 32 to 40. Mark is a physicist and teaches science. He graduated from University College, London and has only been a full member of the Focolare Movement (i.e. a *focolarino*) since 1988. This is his first focolare. He is a Catholic. Mike teaches R.E. and is an Anglican. Callan who is also an Anglican, works full time for New City, the publishing press of the movement in England. He is something of a poet, a student of religions with a Ph.D. from Lancaster University. He comes from Southampton and worked for some time with Age Concern, as well as Schools Broadcasting at the BBC. He started his work with New

City in 1989. He was ordained Deacon by the Bishop of London in St. Paul's Cathedral in June 1993.

A Spiritual Pilgrimage

Each of these six has his own story to tell of how he found his way into the Focolare Movement. Tomeo was very anti-Franco, which in Spain meant being against the Church and sympathetic to Marxists. His contact with the Focolare Movement showed him people who really lived the Gospel. It was like a conversion. He was 23 when he met the Focolare and was soon caught up in the excitement of it all. His three years in Switzerland seem to have been decisive for him, but his training as a *focolarino* was in a place called Loppiano, where most of them spent two years studying the movement, its spirituality and its way of life. Loppiano is near to Florence and therefore is also a good place to learn Italian. There is no doubt that Italian is the language of the movement. All six referred to Loppiano with affection and gratitude as the place where they really learnt the meaning of the Focolare Movement and how to live the 'Ideal'. Carlo also came from a position influenced much by Marxism and what we used to call 'Euro-communism'. His pilgrimage was from revolution to the discovery of a people who really lived the Gospel. It was no argument that led him to total Christian commitment, but the quality of life he saw among the Focolare people, especially in Loppiano. What clinched his decision was that for these people the Gospel worked. The influence of the Focolare Movement on him at first was to send him back to church and to endeavour to live the Christian life at home.

Mark, the youngest of the team, lost a great deal of his belief in God and the Catholic Church as he studied science. He was then influenced by a girl, who listened to him and seemed to care. She introduced him to some young members of the Focolare Movement – *Gen*, they are called, after the exclamation of Pope Paul VI when he saw St Peter's Square crowded with them – 'a new generation' he said. Mark met these young people and they all seemed to be like her, ready to listen and to understand. Among them, the darkness of his doubts was lit up by light and he saw the beauty of conviction in the lives of these 'Gen'.

Callan had rejected all belief at the age of 14 and he was soon attracted to nature religions, until he was taken to a convention of a special kind – called in Focolare language a *Mariapolis* (city of Mary) – at Middleton, near Manchester. He saw young people trying to love and the emptiness in his life was filled with the longing to be like them. He met the Gospel in living terms and heard experiences of life, which led him to understand the way in which Jesus was forsaken for us and is with us in our hopelessness. The phrase, *'Jesus Forsaken'* is a Focolare message, as is the phrase *'Jesus in the midst'*, which Callan discovered when he was on a retreat. He had a very close friend whose pilgrimage was similar, except that he saw marriage as his vocation, so although he belongs to this focolare in West London, he does not live in the house with them, but at home with his wife and two children.

A Married Focolarino

Paul is 37, English and an Anglican. He is a teacher, who for years taught R.E. and other subjects and is now employed by an Educational Authority to supervise and help in the teaching of religion in its schools. As a student in his teens, he was deeply moved by the poetry of T. S. Eliot and recalls how he recognized himself in the poem 'The Hollow Men'. He was one of them. He tried everything – nature religion, mysticism, Hinduism, Buddhism and then broke down. One day he saw the BBC programme, *A Place called Loppiano*, and began to look for the Focolare. He went to Loppiano for six months and realised that in all the religions he had sought, he had not found one in which the Saviour was prepared to die for him. This thought moved him

and he attended a *Mariapolis*, met its principal music
group, called *Gen Rosso*, of which he was mildy critical,
and yet they had something more than music. He then
went to a meeting at which Igino Giordani was speaking
and learnt from him the vocation of marriage. Igino
Giordani is sometimes referred to as the co-founder
of the Focolare Movement. He had met the founder,
Chiara when she was quite young and became himself
the first married focolarino. Paul met him in 1975, he
married in 1979 and was assigned to this West London
focolare. His wife was assigned to a focolare of women.
This separation is one of the strengths of the Focolare
teaching on marriage, which as Igino Giordani (affec-
tionately called 'Foco' in the movement) says, is not
to complete a person, but is the union of two complete
persons. By belonging each to her and his own focolare,
each brings a total experience of a whole person to
the task of forming a union. With their two children,
they also form their own focolare at home and discover the gift of unity. The children grow naturally
into this unity.

Jesus in the Midst

The unity of a focolare is not achieved by effort, but
by allowing Jesus to be present. His promise can then
be claimed: 'Where two or three are gathered in my
name, there am I in the midst of them' (Matt. 18:20).
If there is any threatened disharmony, then the members of the group, in openness and humility, confessing
their contribution towards the disharmony can meet in
Jesus' name: with him in their midst. It was one of the
earliest 'Words of Life' and has remained central in
Focolare spirituality. Although unity is not achieved by
effort alone, it is maintained by holding together all the
aspects of the Christian life in harmony like the colours
of the rainbow. The children of the movement find the
analogy of the rainbow helpful and it is used to teach
them various aspects of Christian life.

The Full Team in West London

The core membership of the focolare in West London is six men, who are resident, and one married focolarino. But that is not the full team. There are also *volunteers* who are not committed to the focolare community in quite the same way, but who nonetheless are trying to live the Ideal and are supportive of the work. In addition there are *clergy*, Anglican and Roman Catholic. There are sixteen volunteers in this focolare and fifteen clergy. This constitutes a formidable unit of Christian resources and they play their part in local affairs. Each focolarino is a loyal and active member of his parish church, as are the volunteers. One example of the involvement of this group of dedicated workers is the part they play – in unity – with 'Christians Together' in their district. The successor to the British Council of Churches, now joined by the Catholics, 'Christians Together in England' depends ultimately upon its local manifestations. The Focolare input, as in many other areas, is considerable. The movement is now an associate member of the national organisation.

The Focolare in South London

While a man fully committed to the Focolare Movement is called a *focolarino*. a women is called a *focolarina*, each with the appropriate Italian changes of ending for the plural: *focolarini* and *focolarine*. One focolare of women lives in a similar house to that of the men, but in a rather noisier area of South London. The complement is as usual six, but there is a complication in that two focolarine were related to two focolare and therefore moved between houses – there are others in London. Only six are resident at any one time, but seven have a strong attachment to the house and there are also two married focolarine. Quite a group – nine devoted women, living in community much as the men are, and trying to live the Ideal. They follow the same 'Word of Life' each month, come together for 'Jesus in the midst', and discover in their sorrows the meaning of identifying with 'Jesus forsaken'. They all

have affectionate memories of Loppiano and at least once
a year they attend a Mariapolis. Their spirituality differs
in no way from that of the men. There is no sexism in the
Focolare Movement.

What strikes one immediately is the ease with which
they entertain visitors and the natural way they talk of
their spiritual experiences. There is no high pressure in
their religion, it is like the air they breathe. Most of the
nine women are in their thirties, with two a little older.

Celia is English, from Yorkshire in fact, and is employed
as a secretary in the office of the Catholic Archdiocese of
Southwark, working for Bishop Henderson, who has special responsibilities for dealing with relations with other
religions. This gives her scope to use the special gift of the
Focolare Movement which is unity. In 1973, when she was
a teenager, she was persuaded to attend a Mariapolis but
everything seemed to go wrong. She even lost her luggage.
However she noted how these people at the Mariapolis
dealt with crises. They cared and helped, they did not
panic; Celia was impressed. The majority were Catholics
like herself, but she saw a difference. Her Catholicism had
been formal and meant going to Mass, while everything
religious happened in church. These people talked about
'The Word' and showed how the Bible, taken little by
little, could be lived. They not only believed in God, they
seemed to know him! In particular she found the Gospels
coming alive for the first time. Three years later she was
taking part in a street theatre in the East End of London
when an IRA bomb went off. There was panic, but not
among the Focolare. They infused a sense of peace into
the fear and hatred caused by the explosion. Later Sheila
Cassidy influenced her, as she read how she had suffered
in Chile and said to God that she was prepared to give
him a blank cheque on her life. The double influence of
Sheila Cassidy and the Focolare people led her in her
early twenties to offer that blank cheque to God. She
enjoyed the activities of the movement as a 'Gen' and
was led to further dedication. In 1980, seven years after
she had attended that Mariapolis, she went to Loppiano

for the customary two years and in 1982 was assigned to this focolare in South London where she has been for ten years, with occasional periods in a neighbouring one.

Anne is also English and also from Yorkshire, a little older, a specialist in information technology, working on analytical programmes at Software House. She studied Mathematics and Computer Studies at Liverpool University. She was soon involved with the young people of the movement, in a special work among gypsy children in Liverpool. She met Paul and Callan, (now in the West London focolare) who were involved with the music group of the movement and joined with them in youth activities. What she found most powerful in the movement was the sense of unity. She visited the world headquarters which were then in Rocco di Papa near Rome and was soon convinced that that was where she belonged. She was in Loppiano, 1977–79 and then assigned to a focolare in London. When she moved from that focolare to another it was only across the river. She has been in this South London focolare now for nine years.

Noreen is a Scottish Catholic, the youngest of this focolare. She is a bilingual secretary (French/Italian) and works for a European Bank. She met the movement at fourteen and was not the only one of her family to join. Her brother, who is a priest, worked with the Focolare Movement at its African Centre at Fontem in Cameroun; her sister is a Volunteer. Anne was brought up as a traditional Catholic. She found a new dimension to her religion when she met the movement: God was near and the Gospel was something to be lived, not just read in church. She saw her father changed by this new inspiration and visited the English headquarters of the movement at Welwyn Garden City. There she really began to understand the meaning of 'Jesus Forsaken', not only as Christ on the cross to be worshipped, but a vital part of her own spiritual life. She was trained in Loppiano, 1986–88, and has been three years at this focolare.

Cathy is the oldest; old enough to have felt the impact

of the Second Vatican Council on her Catholicism. It
was like a refreshing breeze. She is a linguist, and the
turning point in her life came in the sixties. Father Green
her confessor challenged her when in college to make a
personal commitment. During her graduate studies in
Belgium, she questioned her faith and was challenged
to a personal commitment again. She knew about the
movement from her mother and recalls a simple story
of a child who did not react when someone pulled her
hair from behind. Such calm acceptance in a child made
her respect the youngest Gen. Her mother went to day
meetings of the movement and took Cathy when she was
21. That was in her home town of Liverpool.

The Focolare Movement has long held an Ecumenical
week in Rome after Easter for Anglicans and some Catholics. She was persuaded to go on this adventure. The week
has an attractive programme. But for her, it went wrong
from the start. They were supposed to fly from Gatwick
but were then transferred to Luton Airport. They then
had to sit up half the night. Of course, she was fuming and
ready to blame anyone in sight. But the rest of the party
seemed calm and at peace, quietly waiting as though no
inconvenience had been caused. The calm impressed her
enormously. Within a short time she was convinced that
the movement was right for her. She went to Loppiano
in 1967 and after her two years training, which always
includes learning Italian, she was assigned to a focolare in
Liverpool for four years. After that, a focolare in London,
some moving around, and now for several years she has
been a member of the focolare in South London.

Sally had a very different story to tell. She is a Catholic
from Belfast. At 18 she was convinced that the Provisional
IRA was right. She hated the British Army who occupied
her streets and persecuted her people. She joined in the
stone throwing. She was beaten up by 'Protestant' youths
who lived near her 'Catholic' area. She saw the 'peace
movements' as ineffective. At her Catholic school, there
was a nun who belonged to the Focolare Movement and
she persuaded Sally to join a school visit to Loppiano.

She was the only girl chosen from that school. The sense of joy struck her and on the last night at Loppiano, she said, 'I am one of these people now.' She returned quite changed. Her family recognized that she now had a real joy within and it showed in all her attitudes. She still held strong views and believed that the structures needed to be changed in the unjust situation of Northern Ireland, but she had rejected violence as a solution to the problems.

A quotation from St John of the Cross, used much by the movement, is 'If you do not find love, put in love and you will find it.' She looked at the situation in Belfast and said, 'The only thing that counts is how much love I put in.' Eventually she went for her training to Loppiano, 1976–78. Her work today is with the Archdiocese of Westminster and she is assigned to the South London focolare but with constant connection with other focolares.

Marie Christine is French. It is characteristic of most focolare that they are international. This one seems heavily weighted on the United Kingdom membership, but even here England, Scotland and Northern Ireland are all represented – together with France. Marie Christine is from a good Catholic family. She first met the movement at a Mariapolis, in 1971, when she was 17 years old. She enjoyed it, but remained a spectator of the movement for four years. Then a letter from a Gen invited her to the Gen Fest held in 1975. A Gen Fest is a mass meeting of the young people of the Focolare Movement, usually in Rome and it is an inspiration. The Gen Fest in 1990 which included many Gen with stories of liberation in Romania, Hungary, Czechoslovakia and other East European countries was televised and had worldwide coverage. It is one of the most exciting gatherings that any young person could attend. Marie Christine is a teacher of mathematics. She was very attracted by Chiara's 'fourth way', which is a 'vocation' to live a life of commitment 'in the world', and in a family. She spent a year in Paris and then went to Loppiano, 1977–79, before being assigned to a focolare in Paris and then another in Toulouse. In both

places she worked as a supply teacher. She has been in
Glasgow and she has travelled much. Now, in the South
London focolare, she works as a teacher of religion and
mathematics to a Sixth Form.

The Married Focolarine

Moira, who, as a married focolarina, does not live in
the house, is an occupational therapist, with additional
specialised clinical work. She was brought up an Anglican
in a strongly evangelical atmosphere. She is another from
Yorkshire. Her father is an Anglican clergyman. She
married in 1971 and has two children. As a girl she had
attended a day meeting, but it was not until 1977 that she
had any lively experience of the movement. She was at
a Mariapolis and observed the life-style of the focolarine
with whom she lived during that week. She noticed how
they helped and cared for people. The message of 'Jesus
Forsaken' took some time to crystalize in her mind. As an
evangelical she knew all about the cross, but the new idea
of transposing the sufferings of Christ into one's own life
moved her deeply. When her husband left the movement
this became particularly significant to her. She worked
through it at the Easter Week in Rome for Anglicans. She
sees now her vocation within the movement is to create
a Christian family and to offer love to her husband and
family. In no way must she allow his separation from the
movement to weaken her marriage.

Breda is also married. She is an Irish Catholic from a
large family. Her mother died when she was in her teens
and the eldest daughter brought up the children. This
sister introduced her to the Focolare Movement and at
16 took her to a Mariapolis. Her discovery during that
week of activity was that the family could be a very
special unit, while at the same time she could be part
of the larger family of the Focolare. She also experienced
a sense of freedom. She joined the Gen in Dublin and her
involvement in the movement began to show and affected
her father. She later developed an interest in one of the

branches of the movement known as the 'New Humanity'. She has her role in this focolare in South London, but also in the wider activity of social and political healing in the New Humanity Movement.

A Summary Observation

There are many focolari throughout the world, but these sixteen we have met are good examples. Each focolare is different, many much more international than these two, but there is a common spirituality. The special gift of unity, which the Focolare Movement is aware of, expresses itself in the unity of the focolari themselves. All these sixteen people have a world-wide circle of friends in the movement, friends with a family likeness. The organisation enables them to meet in a Mariapolis or a Gen Fest, in celebration and in study. The various movements that have been started within the Focolare Movement unite them with the life of the Church (the New Parish Movement), of the community (the New Humanity), of the family (the New Family), etc. There are conferences and events, all of which are like family gatherings, because they all have a common spirituality which is firmly related to life in the world.

One example of the newest expression of the work of the movement will suffice. After Chiara visited Brazil in 1991, she was so moved by the poverty that she decided that the new 'cities' should be developed side by side with the poorest areas. There work would be provided and an economy established which would attract the poor into a 'city' built upon love and unity. Wherever there is distress, the Focolare Movement wants to 'put in love' in order to find it there.

CHAPTER TWO
CHIARA

T he seed of the Focolare Movement lay in the experiences of an Italian girl, born in Trent, 22nd
January 1920. She was still a student when she went
with a party to Loreto, whose most sacred relic is the
little house where Joseph and Mary and Jesus were
said to have lived in Nazareth, transported, according
to the legend, miraculously by angels to the church in
Loreto, Italy. (More rationally, it is explained as built
like a Palestinian house by a family of builders with the
surname, Angel.) The girl's name was Silvia Lubich and
her own words explain what happened:

I was greatly moved when I first entered the little
house at Loreto, set within the great fortified church.
There was certainly no time for me to wonder
whether this was historically the actual house where
the Holy Family had lived. I felt all along immersed
in that great mystery, and although it was unusual
for me, I wept almost continuously as I thought of all
that might have happened there: the Annunciation,
the return from Bethlehem by way of Egypt, the life
of those three: Jesus, Joseph, Mary.

She touched the stones and wooden beams with reverence,
imagining the house built by Joseph. She could hear
the voice of the child Jesus and thought she saw him
crossing the room. She gazed at those walls which had
been privileged to echo with the voice and songs of Mary.
During that student visit, she took every opportunity

to rush into the little house, where she always felt overwhelmed by a divine atmosphere.

'This was contemplation,' she said, 'prayer and in a very direct way, simply life together with those three. It was unforgettable.'

When she returned to Trent, the priest asked her how she had fared and she replied at once, 'I have found my way!' 'Which?' he asked, because there were three possibilities: to enter a convent as a nun; to be the mother of children in the warmth of a family; or live a life of holiness in the world. 'None of these, but a fourth way,' she replied. This fourth way can best be described as 'living as God's family in the world'. It had all the elements of the other three in it: set apart like a nun; the warmth of a family; and a way of holiness in the world. She did not fully understand at first what she was describing, but she knew that it would show to all the world what God had intended for his children in the world. It would be a model of God's way to renew humanity, in preparation for the coming of his kingdom, or rule on earth. All this took time to realise fully, but at 19 she was sure that this 'fourth way' was for her.

The Birth of the Focolare Movement

On 7th December 1943, Silvia confirmed this 'fourth way' by consecrating herself to God. It was her marriage to God and she changed her name from Silvia to Chiara. Only she and her confessor knew of the vow she was about to make at the time, although she has explained it countless times since to the young focolarine. I have described what happened on that day in December 1943 in my biography of Chiara.[1] It was a dramatic December morning, windy and wet following a night vigil in her own house. Dramatic as that story is, she brings out the true meaning of it when she explains her inner feelings at this marriage:

Imagine a young girl who is in love, with a love

which is her first love, the purest one, a love still undeclared, but which begins to burn in her soul. While a young girl in love sees her beloved and experiences him, through her senses, through her body, this girl doesn't see him, doesn't hear him, doesn't touch him or sense his fragrance, at least not with her bodily senses. She senses his fragrance with the senses of her soul, through which love enters in and invades her whole being.

There is no doubt about the joy which Chiara felt.

This experience came four years after the conviction on her return from Loreto that her way was the 'fourth way'. It was all so unplanned. One morning she was taking a bottle of milk to help someone, and feeling good; then, without any warning, she felt with an unexpected clarity that a voice was calling to her: 'Give yourself to God.' She thought she had already done this after Loreto. But something more was required and, as though to convince her, something like grace flooded her soul and she felt that a flame had been lit. Some time later, other girls joined her who understood. These girls were mostly her own age, perhaps younger, one was only 15. In the air-raid shelters they discovered the Gospels and began to try to live out what Jesus said. They served the poor, learnt how to love one another, each asking the other if she was prepared to die for her. They read the Gospels now as they had never read them before. They were not just remote 'Holy Gospels' any more, but words for living.

There was real poverty in Trent and they went to serve the poor, as though they were serving Christ. Trent soon came under heavy bombardment from the Americans and then from the Germans. The crucial moment came on 13th May 1944. There was a particularly heavy bombardment and Chiara and her family fled to the high ground above the town. That night her family decided to leave Trent for a safer part of Italy. Chiara had to make a decision – choose between two families. With the girls she had found another family – the family of God in the world. She chose to remain with them in Trent, keeping a promise she had made to her spiritual father: so they formed the first focolare in the ruined city of Trent.

A New Community of Love

Other girls gathered around Chiara over the next months of the war. They were in various stages of commitment, but all sought to live the Ideal, putting God first, replacing all their previous ambitions. For his sake, they served the poor, they prayed and read the Gospels together in the air-raid shelters and as they read, they discovered new truths and immediately translated them into everyday living. They seemed to be organised by no human plan, but were simply open to the Holy Spirit who directed them. Chiara had received a gift of the Spirit, a very special grace, whose charismatic nature was to be totally open to the Holy Spirit, uniting those who were around her, and above all spreading love like bush fire. The nature of their life together led to a community very like that first community described in the Acts of the Apostles. They were always being surprised as the Spirit led them step by step into a new discovery of love. As they were daily aware that a bomb could end their lives and they would meet Jesus, they tried to discover what mode of behaviour would please him most. Their constant reading of the Gospels led them to the conclusion that Jesus had given them only one commandment, which took precedence over all else, 'to love one another'. They knew that God had loved them so much that he sent his Son to die for them. So they had to be ready to die for one another. With this, Chiara says, 'there came a kind of conversion to our souls, because by now we had the firm conviction that our life must be based upon mutual and continuing charity'.

These girls were devout Catholics already and went to Mass regularly, but now they read, 'If your brother has aught against you, leave your gift at the altar and go and be reconciled to your brother'. That reconciliation came before everything – before school, before going to work, before going to sleep at night. As they went to Mass together, the warning of Jesus came to them and they asked each other, 'Are we ready to die for each other?' But they did not live only at this dramatic level of death. Day by day they lived for each other, sharing both suffering and joy. The Gospels and the Epistles were a revelation to them in many ways, as they discovered they were startlingly practical. The words of the New Testament were not only revered as 'revealed truth', but as practical guides for everyday life. They left the narrow confines of 'religious' and became 'Words of Life'.

'And these words,' wrote Chiara, 'seemed unique to us, so much so that all others, even those in spiritual books, seemed watered down by comparison.' The others gathered around Chiara, who from the beginning was seen to be the one who had received a very special gift from God, in which they shared so long as they were together. It was like an extended and undramatic Pentecost. A little flame descended and one small fire burnt in each life. These flames were the words of Jesus, which linked them together like little fires catching their heat and light from other fires until one great fire blazes.

The First Focolare

These girls, growing up into young ladies, decided to live together as a family, following Chiara's 'fourth way'. Their home was not called a 'focolare' at first, but a *casetta* (little house). The address was Piazza Cappuccini 2, in Trent. It was an apartment consisting of two rooms and a kitchen, situated beneath the church in a little piazza. There Chiara lived and one by one the girls came to live with her. When the number grew they had to find other and larger premises. Those earliest companions have become legendary in the movement: Natalia, Giosi, Graziella, Valeria, Dori, Gisella, Ginetta ... and later others. One of those who came later was

Lia, who has given us a simple, but vivid description of Chiara, as she saw her on the first visit to that apartment. At the end of the war in Europe, 8th May 1945, Lia met a young lady who told her about a girl she had met in the air-raid shelter. As she spoke, Lia's interest was aroused. The young lady gave her Chiara's address:

> I went there the following day. In the kitchen, there was a girl ironing. She greeted me and having put down the iron, stretched out her hand and told me her name was Chiara. Her glance impressed me deeply and I knew that I wanted to stay in that house always.

Lia returned frequently to Piazza Cappuccini after that first visit, and she has described the influence of Chiara:

> She did not talk to me about doubts and compromises, but rather introduced me to a whole new sphere of interests, throwing open the doors of my soul, putting me in familiar contact with God in heaven and God on earth, helping me to discover Jesus in everyone with whom I came into contact.

Lia comments that a 'new ideal' had filled the hearts of these girls, just when the end of the war had left an emptiness. She tells a story of a meeting during those early days:

> When I think about it now, I don't believe that I was invited, but that did not matter. Chiara greeted me warmly. With her were four or five other girls, seated on a blanket, spread out over the polished wood of the floor in a modest room. Soon they began to talk of St Clare of Assisi; but it seemed to me that they were not talking about the same story as I had until then considered to be a legend of ancient

times. After her flight in the night from her parents'
home, the Franciscan whom she had come to meet
asked what she desired. St Clare of Assisi replied
with one word, 'God'. That word came with such
strength from Chiara that it banished space and
time. I realised that that ideal of life was possible
also for me, because Chiara had made it her own
and shown it to me in her life.

The rich young Lia felt that God had invited her to
leave everything: a comfortable life-style, money, all.
From then on, after a short period continuing with her
family, Lia lived the new life, twenty-four hours of the
day, with Chiara and the others. She was a great help
to the focolare and enabled them to spread out beyond
Trent, as more and more of the focolarine went to live
beyond their own city of Trent into the region of Trentino
and focolare were established also in Florence, Rome,
and Milan. All carried the inspiration of Chiara, the first
protagonist for the 'adventure of unity'. Lia took it later
to South America.

The First Married Focolarino

It was not long before men were forming focolares just
like the girls. But within a Catholic culture, the high
view of virginity and celibacy almost assumed that every
member of such an idealistic movement within the church
would be unmarried. The first shock came early with
Igino Giordani, a politician, a journalist, and a married
man with a family. Chiara met him in September 1948,
in the Italian Parliament in Rome. Although a politician,
Igino Giordani was a deeply spiritual man. He longed to
express his full commitment to God within the Church,
but found that the laity were always assigned a second-
class status. Surely, he thought, piety is possible in the
married state. He was already growing tired of the
compromises and half-lies of politics, when one day
a group of religious people, Franciscans, arranged an

appointment with him. His diary, which was very much a diary of self-examination, records the meeting on 17th September 1948:

> This morning, at Montecitorio, I was called upon by angels: a Capuchin, a Friar Minor, a Conventual Franciscan, a man and a woman belonging to the Third Order: the woman is Silvia Lubig who is launching a community at Trent.

(Giordani had not yet learnt to spell her name correctly.) There was an immediate rapport between Chiara and Igino. The spiritual progress of Chiara up to that meeting in 1948 and that of Igino were like plants grown in different soils, but it is remarkable how close their resultant spirituality was. Chiara was 28 and Igino in his 54th year. She came in the glow of a focolare movement among young women with utter devotion to the Ideal; he met her as his political career which had been distinguished was growing sour on him. Both were devout Catholics. That September day in 1948 was a meeting point of God's plans for two of his children. Although it was a revolutionary step which Igino took when he became the first married focolarino and it certainly changed his life, and opened up new vistas for the movement, it nonetheless happened so naturally. This too is characteristic of the Focolare Movement and of Chiara. When he asked if he could be a focolarino she did not hesitate to say, 'Yes'. This uncomplicated way of deciding upon a totally new issue with confidence is part of Chiara's attraction. It comes out even more clearly in the way Igino Giordani described it years later; in an interview:

> I asked directly, 'Couldn't I be part of your community?' 'Why not?' was the reply. 'We want to be Christians as the Church wants us to bear witness to Christ; that's all. You can do it too; come and join us!'

She hardly realised at the time what a radical step she had taken. They soon found his joining gave the possibility of a new breadth to the movement. What attracted him, I think, was the naturalness of this Christian young woman, who had none of the complications that he had met with, among the high dignitaries of the Church. As a married man and a politician, many within the Catholic Church at that time, would have thought of him as being 'excluded from many Christian virtues'. He was a very distinguished man, who had risen in his political career, a man of integrity, respected as an undoubted anti-fascist, a good churchman and the librarian who had catalogued the Vatican Library giving to this oldest library the most modern cataloguing system. In his library work he had sheltered endangered anti-fascists including Alcide de Gasperi, and provided a relatively safe haven for the Christian Democrats to prepare their future government of Italy. It can be said that Igino gave to this young lady, with her charisma of unity, the opportunity to give it to the world. Much of the later development of the movement depended upon the experience that Igino Giordani brought to Chiara. But he would say that she brought much more to him. Giordani's presence in the heart of the movement encouraged a reaching out to apply the spirituality evidenced in the life of Chiara and those who followed her in 'living the Ideal' to the renewal of family life as well as the renewal of society. Giordani strengthened the lay character of the movement. He was soon most aware of the charisma of unity which Chiara brought and put a great deal of his energy into developing the Centre for Unity (Centro 'Uno'), a Catholic contribution to the ecumenical movement made possible by the Second Vatican Council in which the Focolare Movement was much involved.

The Priest in a Lay Movement

Some twelve years later the Second Vatican Council set in motion a renewal throughout the Catholic Church and had its influence among other Christian bodies also. Pope Paul VI, who had to carry through the greater part of the Council after the death of Pope John XXIII, saw the value of the Focolare Movement. Gradually the movement spread out into many areas of life and formed organisations for renewal, using the adjective 'New' in all of them: New Families, New Parishes, New Humanity etc. This tree had twenty-two branches in all. But even before the Second Vatican Council, it was obvious that renewal also required the renewal of priests. In Protestant churches too we know that renewal is more effective in the church if it can carry the ministers with it! The Focolare Movement at the beginning was a movement within the Roman Catholic Church and there the priest is central. The first steps came in Trent once a men's focolare had been assembled in 1948. Inevitably one or other of these men would have a vocation to the priesthood. The first was Pasquale Foresi. He started as one of the earliest *focolarini* with all the new life that comes to those in the movement from living the Gospel day by day, twenty-four hours out of twenty-four hours! When he became a priest he co-operated with Chiara and became the ecclesiastical assistant to the movement. Chiara was always insistent that the movement should be obedient to the hierarchy. She had no desire to lead a break-away movement, even though many of the things she said and did must have appeared very radical to more traditional priests. Foresi helped enormously in those early days to keep relations good with the priests and even to enlist many within the movement. After the Second Vatican Council, he was appointed, by the Holy See, Adviser to the Congregation for the Clergy, especially to study the uneasiness among the priests which was inevitable as a result of the radical changes effected by the Council.

Other priests later came from the Focolare Movement and others joined or associated themselves with the movement when they saw how a group of people, men or women, devoted to the 'Ideal' could renew a parish.

Eventually, a centre was set up just outside Rome to help
bring the spiritual emphasis and the living faith of the
movement to the service of the priests, many of whom
had lost their sense of vocation, or were confused by the
rapid changes brought about by the Council. These were
matters which the priests had to study among themselves.
Meetings were arranged for priests, organised by one of
those twenty-two branches of the Focolare tree, called the
'Priests' Movement'. Such meetings are now held in every
part of the world the movement has reached.

Difficulties with the Hierarchy

In the early years, before the Council, there was a small
group of enthusiastic priests in the Focolare Movement.
They were difficult to classify. They were not an Order,
nor too obviously a movement, and there was nothing
in the structure of the Catholic Church which fitted
them. They certainly seemed to narrow the gap between
priests and laymen, with whom they associated. They
were not protesting against anything and did not form
pressure groups to obtain anything. They responded to
the question, 'What do you want?' with the apparently
naive answer, 'We don't want anything except to be
Christians'. As the priests spent more time with the
focolarini, trying to live as they did, sharing the joy of
knowing that Jesus was in their midst, living in mutual
love and seeing Jesus in each other, there were those
who looked upon them with disfavour and suggested
that this was a deviation from the priestly ideal. In
1960, as a result of complaints that these priests were
caught up in an 'enthusiastic' movement to the detriment
of their priestly function, they were forbidden not only
to belong to the movement, but even to attend any
of its meetings. There were 400 priests in all and it
seemed like a repetition of worker-priests in France
who had earlier been recalled to their altars because
they identified with the workers. Those priests who had
known the joy of, and learnt so much from, the focolarini

were badly shaken and felt a terrible sense of loss, but they obeyed.

Father Pasquale Foresi, focolarino and priest, consulted the ecclesiastical authorities to find a solution. It was then decided that a branch for priests should be formed within the Focolare Movement, but separated from the lay focolarini to maintain the priestly distinction. They have however learnt how to play a full part in the life of the movement. A positive outcome of this difficulty was the formation of a School for Priests within the Focolare Movement.

Don Pasquale Foresi was an important figure in the movement, which he joined at the end of 1948 in Trent. His father, Palmiro Foresi, was a Deputy in the Italian Parliament, a Christian Democrat. Pasquale quickly found his role in the movement, becoming responsible in 1950 for the administrative centre in Rome when he was only 21. He studied philosophy and theology in Rome, completing his studies at the Lateran University as a Doctor of Theology. He was ordained in 1954. He played his part in persuading the hierarchy that the movement was not a deviation. He has published a number of theological and spiritual books and had a share in the development of the publishing firm attached to the movement, Città Nuova (New City). That word 'New' again! He and Giordani have helped to establish the fortnightly journal of the movement (also called *Città Nuova*) as one of the most prestigious journals in Italy. The articles in *Città Nuova* are not all religious; many are influential in determining attitudes towards art, literature, film, music, theatre and politics.

Chiara at the Centre

There are others beside Igino Giordani and Pasquale Foresi who have flanked Chiara in her world-wide work for unity, that in a series of interviews with her has been called 'The Adventure of Unity'. There is Enzo Maria Fondi, born in 1927, who became a member of the

first focolare in Rome in 1950. He practised medicine for
ten years, two of which were in the Catholic hospital in
Leipzig. In 1964, he was ordained priest with the specific
intention of working for the movement. He now has co-
responsibility with Chiara, with special responsibility for
the spiritual formation of the movement and dialogue
with other religions.

Chiara is at the centre of it all. The others have their
responsibilities and they are remarkable personalities –
many of them, but no one doubts the unique role of Chiara
as founder and president.

I remember describing her in 1977 for her biography
and as I read it now I have little to add. She is older
and has achieved much, but she is essentially the same
gifted person:

> She fits no stereotype. She is slight, almost fragile at
> times; yet she is full of life, the life almost of a child.
> She bears a great *charisma*, burdened sometimes by
> it; yet she resists the pious phrase or saintlike look.
> She has suffered much and those closest to her are
> most aware of this; and yet she has a peace and
> quiet which seems to indicate perfect health, only
> the cold hand and slight tremble betrays this first
> impression. She is clearly a very great person, or
> as she would prefer, the bearer of great things
> from God, striking any visitor with a sense of awe
> and privilege at being in her presence; yet, she is
> charming, winning you over by her gracious reaction
> and evident love. She is a real person and you could
> wish there were more like her.

Some fifteen years later, that description still fits. She
is now a recognised world figure, whereas in 1977 when
she was awarded the Templeton Prize, she was little
known outside the Focolare Movement. Since then she
has spoken to millions outside her movement:

On 28th December 1981, Chiara spoke in the Sacred
Hall in Tokyo to 10,000 Japanese Buddhists, with scores of

monitors outside conveying her message to the thousands more who could not find a place. She spoke simply of her experiences in Trent and the Focolare Movement which came from them.

On 31st March 1990, she joined the Pope in sending a message around the world by satellite on the occasion of the Gen Fest in Rome.

During the Gulf War in 1991, she launched a chain of prayer for peace which was taken up at noon every day by 1¹/₂ million people who paused in their work to commit the world to God.

She has talked with the great. She has joined the hands of warring factions, she has brought Christians of different traditions into loving conversation, she has spoken across the boundaries of different religions in peaceful dialogue. Her gift of unity has bound together those who thought themselves irreconcilable.

These events have not changed her greatly. She has matured, looks older, rests more often now she is in her seventies, but the vitality has not diminished. She can still light a flame. When Franca Zambonini was interviewing her as recently as 1991, she asked Chiara about the place of women in society. Chiara has always taken Mary as her model and urged focolarine to do what Mary did: give Christ to the world. Was Chiara a feminist? All her answers were rooted in the Bible:

On the day of Pentecost, the Spirit descended upon all, men and women. The words of the prophet were fulfilled, 'Your sons *and your daughters* shall prophesy.' From all the reports of Christ with women, there emerges a fundamental parity between women and men.

The statutes of the movement clearly state that the President should always be a woman. A priest will usually be a co-president beside her. Today, the co-president is Antonio Petrilli, who was closely associated with Igino Giordani in their focolare until Igino's death. When

reminded of the tremendous growth of this movement
with its branches in every field and on every continent,
the extraordinary fruit of her work, she replied with no
mock modesty, but simple truth: 'we are only a small
hand which helps the Church to realise the programme
of Jesus: that all may be one.'

CHAPTER THREE

THE VIRGIN MARY

There is probably no aspect of spirituality which has divided Catholics and Protestants more sharply than different attitudes to the mother of Jesus. There are historical reasons which need not be rehearsed. Protestants tend to think that Catholics make too much of Mary, wrongly asserting that she replaces Jesus Christ at the centre of devotion and is lifted beyond the human race to the status of a goddess. All this can be based upon observation of primitive expressions of the Catholic faith, but more often simply on prejudice and oft repeated stories. If we are to understand the central place occupied by Mary, the mother of our Lord, in Focolare spirituality, we shall need to disabuse ourselves of such prejudice and simply listen. This is not to deny that there are examples to be found of popular 'religion-like' worship of Mary who is often no more than a good-luck charm. Sometimes it is true that Catholics give us the impression that Mary is a necessary intermediary between us and Christ. This is not true Catholicism, although it can be practised as such. It is certainly not found in Chiara or the Focolare Movement. It may also be necessary to admit that as Protestants we have been influenced by these prejudices to the extent of neglecting the important role that Mary played in the drama of salvation.

When a focolarina makes Mary her model, she thinks of that self-effacing mother who cared for Jesus as a child and brought him up with tender wonder. She also tries to do what Mary did, 'give Jesus to the world'.

Protestants lose a great deal of the feminine side of God

by jettisoning anything and everything to do with Mary. Feminism within the Protestant churches would no doubt have taken a very different form if Mary had been more central in our faith.

Mary of the Gospels

When the young Silvia Lubich came into the 'little house' in Loreto, it was not the Queen of Heaven that attracted her adoration, but the family of three – three virgins, she called them. Mary was the housewife in that sacred home.

The whole Focolare Movement arose out of a re-discovery of the Gospels in the air-raid shelters of Trent. When focolarine turn with affection and gratitude to the statues of Mary in the Catholic churches they visit, it is not to worship her, but to remember one who is their ideal woman. They do not depend upon legends or miracles to assure them of the importance of the mother of our Lord. The Gospels are enough, and their experience of her influence upon them.

The secret of Mary's role in this movement is found in the Gospels and is crucial. Chiara defined it in a talk given in June 1971, entitled 'Mary, Model of Perfection'. Ten years earlier, she had taken the text, 'Be ye therefore perfect, even as your Father which is in heaven is perfect' (Matt 5:48). She was not content with the obvious exposition of the text, that 'perfect' means 'fulfilled', nor would she accept it as for exceptional Christians only. It was the will of God for all Christians. All were to be perfect. Her model of perfection was this woman of Nazareth, Mary. The Spanish contemplative, St Teresa of Avila, had said that the life of the soul, like that of the body, goes through various stages of growth and decay. Each stage has its own characteristics. Each stage has its own trials sent by God and each trial brings its own grace once it has been overcome. It was this which led Chiara to see that the movement would not only contribute to the fulfilment of the prayer of Jesus, 'that they all may be one', but also bear witness to the Christian vocation to 'sanctity'. The focolarine went on loving as Jesus had taught and new light came to them. He revealed to them that the pattern of their sanctity should be found in Mary; not the Mary of ecstatic visions, but Mary's life as described in the Gospels. Although she was extraordinary, the events in her life can be paralleled with the stages in our own spiritual growth.

The name of the movement is now said to be the 'Focolare' and that perfectly describes those homes of focolarine and focolarini; but the original and basically still the name of the movement is *'Opera di Maria'* (Work of Mary) and her name appears again in the exuberant and lively gatherings, like holiday camps, which are held every year, often more than once – the Mariapolis, or city of Mary.

In that talk given on 15th June 1971, 'Mary, Model of Perfection', Chiara outlined the stages of Mary's life as parallels to stages in our own spiritual growth.

The Nine Stages in the Life of Mary

1. The chosen vessel for the birth of the Incarnate Word of God. It is the courtesy of our God that he asks and awaits our response, like one standing at the door knocking. God chose Mary, not just any woman, but a girl who was prepared. All the pictures of the Annunciation show the angel as though conferring a privilege upon this saintly girl, but the Gospels paint no romantic pictures of a princess receiving an angel. Mary is in no palace. She is a girl from Nazareth who would later be surprised when kings (or rather magi) visit her. The Gospel story is quite simple. A virgin is told by a messenger from God that a child will be born in her, who is the child of God. Mary does not fully understand, but she says, 'Yes' to God. From that moment something new was born in her: the physical life of Jesus began in her womb. Chiara bids us learn that in our lives, there are those who come to us as the angel came to Mary, and by their lives or by a

challenging word they speak, we are offered some task for
God, or the dedicating of our whole life. If, like Mary, we
say 'Yes' to God, something new is born in our lives too.
Then, Chiara says, 'Christ could truly begin to develop
and grow mystically in us.'

2.   The second event in the life of Mary was the visit
to Elizabeth. It is clear that she went, to help the older
woman, who even though well beyond the age of child-
bearing was to have a child, because she stayed until
Elizabeth's child was born. Perhaps she also wanted to
talk with her about the strange happening in her own
life. Elizabeth recognised at once what had happened –
'Who am I that the mother of my Lord should visit me!' It
must have been a wonderful, human assurance for Mary.
The Magnificat was the response to this happening. There
are those who question whether it was the song of Mary
or of Elizabeth. It matters little. Certainly, the Focolare
do not argue about that. They see their pattern in Mary's
action rather than her words. Those who have chosen God
as their Ideal, who have said 'Yes' to God as Mary did,
feel that they must begin to love in order to put their
choice into practice. As Mary did to Elizabeth, they
approach those who are in need with an offer of help,
to share their joys and sufferings. Sometimes those in
need recognise that they are being offered more than
help, they are offered a person who loves and cares. It
is possible that the one who is helped will see something
in the helper, even more clearly than he or she knows.
And that can change a life, as the presence of Mary's
embryo child sanctified John the Baptist in the womb
of Elizabeth. There is a story told of a focolarino who
convinced a group of dialectical materialists but he could
not understand what he had said to accomplish so great
a thing. When they were asked what had changed their
philosophy so radically, they replied, 'We have seen the
revolution of Christ in the small miracle of one person'.
He had simply loved them.

3.   The third event in the life of Mary is the birth of
Jesus, whom she offers to the world. This lies at the heart

of Focolare spirituality. Christ had commanded them to love one another. When they did this they experienced that kind of love among themselves which brought the fulfilment of his promise that 'where two or three are gathered together in my name there am I in the midst of them' (Matt 18:20). This can happen in their home, but it can also happen in the factory or office or street, in fact anywhere. Where Christ is spiritually present among two or three, husband and wife, worker and manager, colleagues at work or friends at home, the Gospel brings about a communal life of such quality that the spiritual presence of Jesus can be offered to the world, as Mary gave him physically to the world.

4.   The presentation in the Temple is the next event. Simeon declares his faith in the child as God's salvation in the familiar words of the *Nunc Dimittis*, but he adds a warning to Mary of sorrow to come. 'a sword will pierce through your own soul also'. The focolarina saw in this the warning that, after the enthusiasm for the revolution of the Gospel, suffering must be faced. That is the beginning of understanding suffering: Mary cannot forget those words. Her life will, throughout, be accompanied by a suffering which is inevitable – right up to the cross – and beyond. The Focolare have always recognised necessary suffering as an important element in spiritual development. If anything creative is to occur in the spiritual (and one could say also, in the mental) life, it will inevitably be accompanied by suffering – creative and redemptive suffering, which for one who seeks to live the Ideal is inescapable. At first we are drawn to the revolution of Christ with enthusiasm, but something tells us – a word in conversation, a reading, a talk, a text from the Gospels – that the choice of God as the Ideal has an indispensable condition. Jesus warned his disciples of it: 'Woe to you, when all men speak well of you' (Luke 6:26). The disciples were repeatedly told that the world would treat them as it had treated their Master. We begin to learn gradually about our relationship to Jesus the Crucified, and Jesus the Forsaken. If we are to give

Jesus to the world, as Mary did, we have to learn like her
to say 'Yes' to God for the second time – the 'Yes' of the
cross. When Jesus said that a disciple must 'take up his
cross', he meant it.

5.   Soon after hearing this warning of suffering from
Simeon, Mary experienced it in a very painful way –
the flight into Egypt – leaving behind the blood-stained
persecution of the Innocents. Chiara found in this flight
into Egypt a parallel to her own experience with the
movement.

> The Ideal that we show the world through our
> movement is in conflict with the world, because
> Jesus is a contradiction of the world. For this reason
> when the Ideal begins to spread in a city or in a
> country, the first reservations or criticisms soon
> arise, often from people who find the movement a
> rebuke to their luke-warm Christianity. For us this
> is the moment when we have to take all necessary
> steps to protect our movement as Mary protected the
> infant Jesus by her flight into Egypt. In what we
> do we must remain closely united with the Church
> authorities, following their instructions. At the same
> time we must pray for and love all those who are
> against us and want to stop us.

6.   When Jesus was twelve years old, his parents lost
him in the temple. We can learn from Mary's words
how distressed she was: 'Son, why have you treated
us so? Behold, your father and I have been looking
for you anxiously' (Luke 2:48). Chiara compares this
to a tendency she has noticed among those who seek
to follow the Ideal. After a time they find the old
temptations reappear. They thought they had overcome
them by special grace given to them. She says that these
temptations usually attack patience, charity and chastity.
They cast a shadow over the light that God has given us.
It is then that the lover says to God, 'Why did you leave?

Your presence had become so strong in my soul, that I
felt I could overcome the world with you. Now I am in
the darkness of your absence.' In such a situation, God
gives us the answer that Jesus gave his mother. 'Did you
not know?' Mary had suffered the experience of losing
Jesus. Our 'night of the senses', when we are suffering
the absence of God, is parallel to it. For Mary, it was a
preparation for the time when she would lose her boy
altogether, but not before she had spent some long years
with him. So it is with us. If we can accept the absence
of God, our 'night of the senses' and live through the
darkness of his withdrawal, we can overcome future
absences and temptations with the grace of God, going
on to live long in union with our God.

7.   Mary was there at the beginning of Jesus' ministry,
at the marriage feast in Cana of Galilee; she heard him
preach, saw his miracles of healing and the calling of his
disciples. There is little in the Gospels about her role in
his ministry. She watched and 'pondered all these things
in her heart'. The focolarino is encouraged to witness the
spiritual miracles and the graces accomplished by Jesus
in the midst. The focolarina also watches Jesus drawing
followers to himself and the building up a community.
The disciple of Jesus does not look for the centre of the
stage, but quietly watches the achievements of his or her
Master, overjoyed if some little part of his or her activity
can be taken up in the prime role of Jesus in the midst.
There is much to learn from Mary's silence.

8.   It is at the foot of the cross we find her at the
end of that ministry. There she reaches her hour of
sacrifice and it had been so often foreshadowed that it
was no surprise. An expected sorrow, however is no less
a sorrow. The most tragic moment for her is the word of
separation: 'Woman, behold, your son; son, behold your
mother' (John 19:26–27). Jesus releases Mary from her
motherhood; she is required to renounce her special claim
as mother. That lesson she had learnt in less dramatic
circumstances, when she sought entry into the house
where he preached and heard him say, 'Who is my

mother?'. She had to let him go. He belonged to the
world, for his Father had so loved the world that he
gave him. This is the 'dark night of the soul'. No one
around that cross could have felt the pathos of that cry,
'My God, My God, Why hast thou forsaken me?', as she
did. She was the first to understand, 'Jesus Forsaken'.

When God has any special task for us to do he usually
sends to us at the appropriate moment some trial that
is for us too 'the dark night of the soul'. It is to show
us who we are in our 'useless and unfaithful service' to
God. Anything we achieve must be seen as 'God in us'
accomplishing the work. With such trials, such a night
of the soul, God enables the greatest of his saints to be
separated from the work he is doing that it might be
seen to be God's work. It is a suffering that cannot be
imagined unless you have experienced it. At such times
the desolate figure of Mary at the foot of the cross speaks
to our condition. Like Mary, we have to learn to say, 'Yes'
again to God.

9.   After the death of Jesus, Mary remains. The time
of following Jesus and ministering to him is over. Her life
work is done. She remains with the apostles over the next
few tragic days. She appears to be in the Upper Room,
but her presence is rarely mentioned. She did not go to
the tomb with the other women to embalm the body. She
did not seek the living, among the dead. After the day of
Pentecost, she is not mentioned again. She withdraws,
having done her great work of giving birth to Jesus and
caring for him as a child. She now loses herself. Perhaps
she learnt the truth of the later words of the Apostle Paul,
'It is no longer I who live, but Christ who lives in me' (Gal
2:20). This, we too must learn.

Spirituality

The Focolare Movement began within the Catholic Church
and brought with it new insights into the role of Mary,
the mother of Jesus, for all of us to learn. It is significant
that the Focolare spirituality approached this by way of

the Gospels and its objective is to unite all Christians in a form of appreciation of the role of Mary which does not divide us. In an article entitled, 'The Focolare Movement and what it can offer to the laity and the religious', Chiara writes about this kind of spirituality and its effect upon the movement:

> . . . as you know, a spirituality in the Church is not a way of living Christianity, but it is Christianity seen from a particular angle. Ours is Christianity seen from the point of view of the 'testament' of Jesus (which means from the Gospels), from the angle of unity, a spirituality which gives meaning to Christian living. But life, any life, which includes the supernatural, the richest and the poorest, develops when it joins with others. The anxious person comes, talking to others of his or her despair. The result is that what becomes much clearer is how the despair can be lived through, especially if lived with others.

After describing the incredible growth of the movement into all aspects of the religious life and into every continent, Chiara continues:

> At the heart of the movement are the focolarine and the focolarini, who most distinctively live life in the communes of their focolare, little communities with a new style, modelled upon the family in Nazareth, always maintaining unity between their members. In the Statutes of the movement is written, in fact, that the rule which must take precedence over every other rule is that the spiritual presence of Jesus must always be maintained among the members. As support for the unity which requires renunciation of those things that might separate one person from another, the focolarini have accepted, although not necessarily life-long, vows of chastity, poverty and obedience. Each focolare thus accepts fully the obligation and participation, according to

its means, with those who are called to offer one total
gift to God.

Difficulties for Protestants

There is no doubt that a Protestant brought up on
the sole authority of the Bible as the Word of God
will have difficulty with Chiara's language. She speaks
the traditional language of the Catholic Church and
some of her phrases arouse all the old prejudices. But
her charisma of unity has helped her to perceive the
difficulties Protestants have. If you examine carefully
the substance of what she says, rather than the Catholic
language in which it is formulated, you will soon come
very much closer to her. And a new spiritual experience
of that magnitude is worth striving for.

For many years, Mary seemed to stand in the shadow
of the movement, despite its name. When in 1947, Chiara
was asked why she did not talk more of Mary, she
replied,

> Mary is the door which leads to God. A door is not a
> door unless it opens for one to go through. The Virgin
> is nothing, just emptiness, self-forgetting, purity –
> all the virtues of the Gospel. She is a creature, and
> a creature who has become nothing, when filled by
> God, is love. A closed door is a wall. Who stands
> at the door does not come to God. The door is for
> Jesus. Unity is directed towards its goal. But who
> has reached the goal most values the means. He
> who loves unity and thus is another Jesus loves
> Mary most.

In those early days of the movement, that is as far as
Chiara went. Mary was in the shadows in order that
Christ might come to the fore.

The New Discovery of Mary

It was in 1949. That year is often referred to as a year
of special grace, of special light, and much growth in the

movement. Chiara called it 'The time of enlightenment in our history'. It led to a new understanding of Mary. Somewhat later this caused the greatest difficulty for Protestants, who saw much in the movement which they valued, but stumbled at this new insight. It appeared to go beyond the Gospels and make Focolare spirituality follow the pre-conciliar Catholic Church in its attitude to Mary. There is great difficulty in accepting the Catholic understanding of Mary as, although a creature, 'the one unique creature held fast within the Trinity'.

When Chiara expressed this she did so in the language of a mystic, with extravagant similes, but she never lost sight of the biblical basis of what she expressed. She went far beyond the Gospel stories, but returned to them whenever she could. Her Catholic inheritance and her experience of the Gospels, in the air-raid shelters, were like point and counterpoint in Bach's music. Read and ponder a translation of what she said:

> And if the Logos, the Word, is the beauty of the Father, then Mary, through whom the Word of God came, was of incomparable beauty. So strong was this impression upon us that to this day (she is speaking in 1972) we cannot forget what we have understood at that time . . . To see her like this drew us to her and exploded in a new love for her. And in the manner of the Gospel, she responded to this new love by showing us who she was: Not only the girl from Nazareth, the most beautiful creature in the world, the heart which contains and goes beyond the love of all the mothers of the world, but: the Mother of God. The slightest intuition of this secret was enough to render us dumb in prayer and thanksgiving that He had wrought so great a thing in a creature. In that moment a new dimension was revealed in our own lives, which until then had remained totally unknown to us.

This new dimension came from a mystical vision which

went beyond the traditional symbolism of Mary. Then
came the secret, beginning from the medieval spirituality
and pressing forward to a new insight:

> We stood astounded before the greatness of Mary as
> if we had learnt to know her for the first time . . .
> Mary is the Mother of God, certainly, because she is
> the mother of the human nature of that person who
> is the Word, who is God become man. One cannot
> separate the Word from the Father and from the
> Holy Spirit. Jesus said to Philip in reply to his
> question, 'He who has seen me, has seen the Father.
> I am in the Father and the Father in me'. Paul says
> of Jesus, who is God, that he emptied himself – and
> that emptying began in the womb of Mary.

Chiara began to understand now why the statue of Mary
stands beside the tabernacle in Catholic churches. In
1972, as she explained this experience of only a few years
before, she tried to apply it in a practical way.

The articles which appear in *Città Nuova* in 1975 and
1976 bring Mary more and more to the front. Their titles
alone illustrate this: 'When Mary became our Mother',
'Being the Mother of Christ', 'Love makes us do as
she did'. Then in a guide to sanctity, she writes, 'Jesus
appears to be a model too high for us to reach. In order to
rise from our littleness to his greatness we need a divine
"inclined plane". Mary is this "inclined plane".' She is a
help, not an intermediary.

Chiara goes back to the Gospel story to show how 'Mary
becomes our mother'. At the foot of the cross, Jesus turns
to Mary and John, giving them to one another. To Mary
he says, 'Woman, behold your son'. It is a substitute son.
In much the same way, every child of God who looks up to
the cross with grateful acceptance for his or her salvation
is cared for. We may recall that Paul saw Philemon as his
son because he had brought him to Christ. Chiara makes
this parallel when she adds: 'The greatest gift that God
can give to anyone is the gift of spiritual maternity or

paternity. We are all able to be fathers and mothers
of souls.' So she appeals: 'Let us imitate Mary, let us
become similar to her.'

The Influence of Mary on the Focolare Leadership

When Chiara was asked in an interview with Franca
Zambonini about the differences the Vatican Council had
made to the place of 'the woman' in the Church, she
recounted a conversation with Pope John Paul II. She told
him one day, when she had mustered enough courage,
that the statutes of her organisation now contained
the requirement that the president should always be a
woman – and she waited for his reply. It came at once,
'Why not?'. In fact he not only approved, but thought it
was the obvious decision to take.

There is little doubt that the Focolare Movement, aided
by the Second Vatican Council, has effected a revolution
in the Church in its attitude to the laity and to women
in particular. By relating this to Mary, Chiara has
been able to accomplish a great deal for women in the
Church without in any way diminishing her respect
for the hierarchy. She has always been obedient to
the demands of the hierarchy, giving to bishops and
popes the authority of the apostles. Again she finds a
text for this in 'He who hears you hears me'. Within
the structure of obedience and orthodoxy she has found
a position of worth and dignity for women in the Church.
She is supported by Paul's words, 'In Christ, there is
neither male nor female.'

What then does she think of the ordination of women?
What she says must be studied carefully because it shows
her high estimate of the place of women in the Church,
without asking for ordination as priests:

As you know, this is a burning question, with
ecumenical implications, especially in relation to
our conversations with the Anglican Communion. I
would like to say first of all that 'the woman' within

the ecclesiastical community bears the heavy burden
of fundamental values, and that God has placed her
there to defend these values, which are inherent in
her special vocation ... It is true that Jesus did
not pronounce on the issue of the ordination of
women or their place in the Church, but he gave
to the Christian woman her incomparable model,
which all the great Christian women in history have
preserved: Mary, his mother. In her, every woman
who wishes truly to serve the Church can recognise
what is to be her duty. Amidst all the baffling
arguments, the Christian woman can understand
that it is not the priest that she is to imitate, because
she has a different task in the Church, which is just
as important and equally indispensable: she must
affirm, in a way that only she can, the value, the
prime value of love, over all treasures, over all other
elements that constitute our religion. She has that
highest dignity, which brings colour back into the
life also of those called to the priesthood. Yes, love
is the most important. We know it: you don't go to
heaven because you are a priest or a bishop. You go
there because you have loved. Even the priests and
bishops, who are the pillars on which Christ has
founded his Church, can in the end find themselves
in hell. But in that place you will find neither men
nor women who have loved.

Love is the most important thing. Again it must
be said that the hierarchy and the clergy are for this
world, while love endures on into the next life. It is
necessary that part of the people of God therefore
affirm this truth without possibility of deception.

It is in supernatural love, it is by love and with
love, that the woman, already by nature woven into
the threads of love, bears every sacrifice in order to
find her place in the Church: minister, as she is, of
these things, across the centuries and even today.
By love she keeps alive the presence of Mary in
the Church ... The ministry of love is perhaps

more fruitful even than the work of the priests and bishops, if we recall the words of Paul: 'Though I give my body to be burned and have not love, I am nothing'. To be ministers of God without love is not according to the will of God. When there is no love, all is reduced to form, and simply ritual. Hence also, 'You are not called to the priesthood', as the Pope said, 'the teaching of the Church is quite clear on this point, which in no way alters the fact that women are truly an essential part of the evangelical design for the proclamation of the Good News of the Kingdom.'

Now Pope John Paul II also said, 'However true it is that the hierarchy is in succession to the Apostles, who were all men, it is also most true that in a charismatic sense, the women take the lead in the Church just as much as the men, perhaps more.'

Those are the words of the Pope! In the encyclical, 'Mulieris dignitatem', he has also said, enthusiastically confirming the words of H. Urs von Balthasar,

'Mary is the Queen of the Apostles without pretending to their apostolic powers. She has other and greater powers Therefore the woman living her vocation to the full, with the faith, nobility and love of Mary, can be the revelation for the Church of that "dimension of the life of a disciple of Christ that is influenced by Mary". She can contribute towards keeping alive and manifesting that influence of Mary which is essential for the Church.'

It is in this way that Chiara can read the controversial encyclical, 'Mulieris dignitatem', as a raising of the status of women in the Church. Her understanding, which she is convinced is also the understanding of Pope John Paul II, is that this encyclical marks a step forward in applying the traditional Catholic view of Mary to exalt the vocation of women in the Church.

CHAPTER FOUR
UNITY

Let us begin with Chiara:

> Unity is the word that sums up our spirituality.
> Unity – which for us contains in itself every other
> supernatural reality, every other practice or com-
> mandment, every other religious attitude.

Chiara has never wavered from that supreme estimate of
'unity'. It came to her at the very beginning and it was
not always easy to understand. Amidst all the difficulties
of those early days, she remembered:

> In our heart one thing was clear: unity is what God
> wishes from us. We live by being one with Him and
> with one another and with all. This splendid vocation
> binds us to heaven and it immerses us in a universal
> fraternity. Nothing is greater. For us there is no ideal
> higher than this.

She was later to discover as of equal importance the
experience of Jesus Forsaken. Both have their roots in the
Gospels. *Unity* comes from the priestly prayer of Jesus in
John 17; *Jesus forsaken* comes from the cry of dereliction
in Matthew 27:46. They cannot be separated for her. In
a letter of 1948, she wrote quite simply and profoundly:

> The book of light which the Lord has written for
> me on my soul, has two aspects: a luminous page
> of mysterious love: *Unity*. A glowing page of sad

mystery: *Jesus forsaken*. These are two sides of a single coin.

For the purpose of understanding them we shall separate them into two chapters, only to bring them together again later.

The Summer Mariapolis

One of the most public demonstrations of the central importance of 'unity' to the Focolare Movement is the Mariapolis. In any district where there are several focolari, a summer rally is held to unify the movement in that area. It goes back almost to the very beginning of the movement, in 1949. The first young women who were attracted to the life of the Focolare began to spend their summer holidays together in the Dolomites, within a reasonable distance from Trent. This holiday 'camp' went on for several weeks and focolarine would come and go according to the dates of their holidays. They were holidays of such wonderful experience with each other that they felt they wanted them to go on forever. They called them 'cities of Mary' (Mariapolises). These days and weeks were opportunities to live the Focolare ideal without distraction of work or from others who might not understand. Gradually over the years they were more closely organised and usually lasted just a week in each district. They are still very precious times for members of the movement, when for a limited period they can live together and practise the art of loving one another. Soon the value of inviting others to share the Mariapolis and taste something of the Focolare way of life became evident. The summer Mariapolis is now organised in such a way as to show a model of the new society for which they strive. People of all ages and professions, priests, laity and members of religious orders, take part in different activities during these days together. They pay particular attention to those who seem far from God or strangers to Focolare ideas. There are many cases of people who have come with Focolare friends to one of these Mariapolises simply because they wanted to share a holiday with them, but while there they have experienced a knowledge of unity which has given them hope in their lives.

The earliest Mariapolis in the Dolomites grew so large that it had to be divided into smaller gatherings. In 1959, for example, 12,000 people attended over a period of three months. Olive Wyon in her survey of post-war spiritual movements, *Living Springs*, tells of her visit to this Mariapolis in 1959, with its representatives from twenty nations speaking nine languages:

> There is nothing 'separatist' or sectarian about this movement. Its members are loyal Catholics, living 'in the world'. They lay great stress on love in action, in daily life as well as in special relationships. It is not easy to describe this movement because it is always on the move. It seems to grow by a sort of cheerful and hopeful infection from one small group to another – all of them determined, as far as they can, to do the will of God to the utmost, to live the Gospel before they preach it. As their name suggests, this movement is a 'Fire' which is spreading by leaps and bounds.

That was the impression of a Protestant visitor, who knew a great deal about spiritual movements. I visited a Mariapolis in 1977 when the movement was already world-wide and talk of the Dolomites was part of its folklore. It was the English Mariapolis that I visited, held near Manchester.

From Tuesday to Saturday, about 600 people, associated in some way or another with the Focolare, with their friends, lived together in La Salle College in Middleton. It was a Teacher Training College, well appointed and in good condition. Some of the members lived in student rooms, although many sleeping-bags were brought in to increase the number who could be accommodated. On the green there were tents and caravans. Everything was well organised and with the minimum of fuss. But I soon realised that although this looked like an over-subscribed conference, such as I had often known at the Conference Centre in Swanwick or High Leigh, it was different. It was not a conference. It was a village. There were families with children playing around the family tents as they might in village streets; there were young people crowded into a visitor's room and talking into the night. Although the kitchen staff began by thinking of this overcrowded meeting as just another conference, they soon discovered the difference. There was an atmosphere of concern for other people. In Focolare language this was 'love'. The way to love the kitchen staff is to get in on time for meals and with very few exceptions they did! It was a happy atmosphere, like a huge well-integrated family. They played games, shared experiences, above all they listened to one another. There was a marked absence of pressurised religion. This was a holiday and the religious element simply found its place.

There were two Masses every morning, one Anglican and one Roman Catholic, held simultaneously. Each prayed for the other and asked forgiveness for the separation. They accepted the discipline of their church, but saw that separation was painful and wrong. A common phrase as two newly found friends separated for their respective Masses, was 'I shall receive for you'. I attended both Masses, and as a Baptist, I belonged to neither, but I appreciated the spirituality of both – and also experienced the touch on the shoulder by a friend who went up to receive and said, 'I will receive for you'. Looking back on my notes made immediately after that Mariapolis in 1977, I found one occasion that most deeply affected me. It was during a session, when the whole Mariapolis was divided into smaller groups – no, not the whole, but just those who wanted to! In the groups, members of focolare began to tell of their experiences. Some spoke of how they had discovered the movement, but what impressed me most was the experience of failure. They were not all success stories. Let me quote from these notes:

Although there are special meetings arranged for
sharing experiences, they are only samples, because
sharing goes on one to one, all the time and all
over the place. This sharing is one of the main
activities in a week of fun and love. Living the
Ideal, you soon learn, is not easy and people need
the support of others who are also trying. One man
confessed that since he married and changed his job,
he had lost the power to love those he works with.
Married life concentrated his energies to such an
extent that he found it impossible to rouse a love
for his new colleagues at work. He was worried,
because he seemed to have lost something. His
wife was in the group with him and she heard
this. She is equally involved in the movement and
they talked their problems through with the group.
What came out was a reminder of what they already
knew, that they had married as whole persons. They
were so close to each other now that they were not
developing the separateness which was necessary
both for their individual spirituality and even for
their marriage.

As I listened to 'confessions' of failure to live the Ideal
by both of these real people, I knew that the Focolare
Movement was true: these admissions of failure to live up
to the Ideal, the struggle, the careful listeners who did not
judge, but tried to help, I was more deeply impressed than
I would have been by a whole series of success stories.
Here were two ordinary people attempting extraordinary
feats in the name of God, not finding it easy, aware of
their failure and yet going on. Most important of all they
knew that they belonged to a supportive family. I was
reminded of Chiara's remark more than once during
that week: 'The focolarini fall down, but know how to
get up again.'

'What is the purpose of these meetings?', Chiara was
asked, and responded at once, 'To work together to make
a more united world, and with that purpose in mind, to

address the problems of society, the family, the world of
youth etc.'

A Sign of the Times

When Chiara expounds what unity means she does not
begin analytically, nor from some mystical, revealed
truth. I have never heard her say, 'that is difficult to
understand'. She looks at the situation as it is and detects
the hand of God in it. When she writes about 'unity', she
begins by pointing out how divided the world is, with its
multiplicity of tensions – between east and west, north
and south, tensions in the Middle East and wars in
Central America. Then she points out that a curious
reaction to this is taking place – there are movements
towards unity everywhere: 'Despite all these tensions,
the world is moving towards unity'. She calls it a sign
of the times and points to commerce, mutual dependence
and even the churches. After centuries of indifference and
even struggle, the Holy Spirit is leading churches and
ecclesiastical movements towards unification. The Second
Vatican Council is one of her prime examples of this. And
Protestants can point to the growth of the ecumenical
movement. Our 'unhappy divisions' may still continue,
but the relation between the various denominations has
changed incredibly this century.

When Chiara looks back to the very beginning of the
movement and the early morning meditations she had in
the first focolare, she is convinced that they were led to
demonstrate above all, the power of love in unity. When
those early focolarine spoke of the necessity to be another
Jesus to those they encountered, they had understood the
programme God had set out for them:

> The soul must, above all else, keep its gaze fixed
> on the one Father of many children; then look at
> all persons as children of one Father. With every
> thought and affection of the heart piercing through
> the barriers that surround the (merely) human life,

let it become an acquired habit to think constantly
of the universal brotherhood in one Father God . . .

Jesus, our model, taught us just two things, which
are really one: to be children of our Father, and to
be brothers and sisters to one another.

It is important to underline a virtue which is essential
for unity with God and with one's neighbour, and which
Paul in his letters indicated when he was stirring up the
Christians to mutual love by building unity. That virtue
which unites the soul to God is humility, self-denial.
One tiny spot of humanity which is not taken up into
the divine by being surrendered to God can destroy
unity, with grave consequences. The unity of the soul
with God presupposes the total annihilation of self,
humility of the highest degree. Unity with other souls,
then, is attained through humility earnestly seeking the
'higher gift' by accepting every possibility of service to
our neighbour. Every soul which desires unity must have
a single-minded purpose: to serve all, because in all one
serves God.

Such reasoning which lies at the heart of the Focolare
Movement finds its clearest exposition in Paul's letters:
'For though I am no man's slave, yet I have made myself
everyone's slave, that I might win more men to Christ. (1
Cor. 9:19)

This verse is followed by precise examples – accepting
the burden of the law in order to win Jews, renouncing
the privileges of being a Jew in order to win the weak.
'I have become all things to all men, that I might by all
means save some.' (v. 22)

That is love, that is humility, that is 'unity achieved
by means of renunciation of all privileges'. Paul reaches
his profoundest renunciation, when in his longing for the
salvation of his own people, he cries out:

Before Christ and my own conscience in the Holy
Spirit I assure you that I am speaking the plain
truth when I say that there is something that

makes me feel very depressed, like a pain that never leaves me. It is the condition of my brothers and fellow-Israelites, and I have actually reached the pitch of wishing myself cut off from Christ if it meant that they could be won for God. (Rom. 9:1–3, J. B. Phillips' translation)

Compromise and Risk

The phrase, 'all things to all men', has often been used in a pejorative sense to mean compromising one's beliefs in order to be accepted by the other. Neither Paul nor the Focolare Movement would use it in this way. The self-denial comes from an inner conviction which is not negotiable, and the humility is based upon a knowledge of worth in the eyes of God – unmerited worth, but worth nonetheless.

D. T. Niles, the Methodist from Sri Lanka, who was one-time chairman of the Evangelism Committee of the World Council of Churches, said, 'You cannot evangelise without coming so close to the other person that you are in danger of losing your faith'.

That was provocative language, but it describes a truth which the focolarini could well understand. If you wish to convey your faith to another by your love it means listening carefully and sympathetically, trying to understand what the other believes. Such understanding and sympathy is dangerous to an ideologue, who protects a fundamentalist's faith. But if you are open, the only protection is the inner conviction of certainty. Truth needs no other protection. The most persuasive argument may leave you without an answer, but a faith built upon experience cannot be destroyed by arguments. All that is at risk then is the mode of expression or the arguments for truth, and these are peripheral. It is this inner certainty born of experience, which may well be open to various kinds of expression, which makes it possible for focolarini or focolarine or indeed the whole movement to discover a unity with Buddhists without loss of faith. For them even unity with the Buddhist, becomes a unity with Jesus in the midst.

There are many centuries of bitter struggle between Catholics and Protestants behind us. At least, I hope they are behind us. In my lifetime, I have seen the change – Oh so slowly! – from prejudice and hostility, to wary conversations, permission to appear on the same platform together, later even to say the Lord's Prayer together, until we are now in an atmosphere of learning from one another. Catholics and Protestants alike have much to learn from each other, but they will only learn if they listen with openness.

Two amusing incidents occur to me from when I had responsibility for religious broadcasting in the BBC. One was when we first televised a Catholic Mass. It was done very carefully as though we were touching explosive material. My inclination was to do most of it in long shot. It was my Catholic colleague, Father Agnellus Andrew, who said, 'No, let us go right up to the altar and see what the priest is doing there.' He was right. Many letters poured in from the Protestants who had had all kinds of prejudiced ideas of what the priest did at the altar. They wrote with surprise that what he appeared to do was not very different from what the Anglican vicar did! They were relieved to find that no diabolic action went on in secret at the altar. No words could have helped clear that mental confusion, but the viewer had switched on and watched, listening and seeing, without prejudice.

The other incident was when an angry evangelical, after a lively Catholic broadcast, wrote to say, 'How dare you let these Catholics preach our Gospel?' I am sure that my colleagues had similar letters from bewildered Catholics who were discovering what Protestants were up to and that they believed very much the same, most of the time, as the Catholics. That was not compromise. Many Protestants learn to enjoy watching Catholics at worship and soon learn that we are both looking towards Jesus. For, basically, our unity lies in the same Jesus. We do not need to fight all the battles of the Reformation over again.

We need to listen from a standpoint of inner security in the experience of our Lord, who is always with us.

Unity is Jesus in our Midst

Unity, then, is Jesus. Yes, the risen Lord said to his disciples: 'Lo! I am with you always, even unto the end of the age.'

Lutheran and Catholic come together. Dietrich Bonhoeffer, in his Christology lectures, said, 'Christ is with us and present in the Church in three different ways — the Eucharist, the proclamation of the Word, and the fellowship created by the Holy Spirit when believers worship together.'

Chiara writes of the unity of the Eucharist, the Word and whoever has the task to evangelise, as the close presence of Jesus in the Church. But she passes away from the discussion of how he is present to the practical task of living in the world as a believer, with whom Christ is present in unity:

> We are called to live this unity every moment of our daily lives. It is realised in serving our neighbour, brother or sister. But how can we best practise this service? From the earliest times it has become clear to us that this can best be achieved by making ourselves one with every neighbour we encounter.
>
> We must be one with our brother, not as an ideal, but in reality; not in the future, but now. To be one is to feel the sensitivity of our brothers in ourselves. It is to deal with their problems as though they were ours, and make them ours by charity. That is to be them. And this for love of Jesus in our brother.

The focolarini are not noticeably evangelists, although they create by their attitude of love and concern an atmosphere in which enquirers ask why they are so ready to help and what it is that motivates them. Many a focolarino has been faced with such a question and then had to think what to say. As in all they do, the Gospel has a word for it. Jesus said, 'When the Spirit of truth comes he will guide you into all truth'. But even more clearly, 'He who has my commandments and keeps them, he it is who loves me; and he who loves me will be loved by my Father, and I will love him and make myself known to him'. (John 16:13; 14:21)

Focolarini testify again and again to the way in which this has worked. They will tell you of many occasions when they have not been able to deal with a question intellectually and yet they have found the very words that met the need. They were quite human words, but they were exactly the right ones. But it is not only the words, it is the making of a relationship. The real concern of the enquirer enters into the person who loves and makes it possible for such a one to give the right answer to the question. Then, between the two persons, this kind of love is established, this ease of mutual comprehension, and thus the unity that brings Christ into the midst is realised.

Living the Word in Unity

On this central idea we must listen to Chiara herself:

> From the beginning, God's programme for the move-
> ment has been this: to make contact with our
> own environment, consuming those around us in
> unity, while at the same time remaining open to
> all others . . .
>
> Just as any object that approaches a whirlpool is
> sucked into it (the suction is caused by the meeting
> of two currents! . . . Isn't this too a symbol of unity?),
> so each person who meets Jesus (the Jesus who is
> among us) will be lost in his love, caught in the
> whirlpool.
>
> On earth we live inserted in the Church militant.
> We cannot wage this war without weapons, nor
> without an objective. Our weapon is Christ, who
> lives in our most perfect unity; our objective, 'that
> all may be one' . . .

The focolarini in a way that is typical of the movement, seek to realise the prayer of Jesus and they believe that it will be realised. They will not have the words of it watered down, nor have it applied to an elite group of disciples. In John 17 Jesus said quite clearly:

> I do not pray for these only (i.e. the disciples) but also for those who believe in me through their word, that they may all be one; even as thou, Father, art in me, and I in thee, that they also may be in us, so that the world may believe that thou hast sent me. (John 17:20–21)

That prayer of Jesus, that dream of Jesus, is the charter of the Focolare Movement. But it does not stand alone. It has other consequences which makes it a fire to light the world.

The Monthly Word of Life

Spirituality is not learnt and then left. It is like a plant that needs constant feeding. So every month, to every focolare, there comes the text for the month. It is chosen centrally and accompanied by a commentary which enables the focolarini to live it out in every aspect of life. You may see it pinned up to remind all in the house of the 'Word of Life' which they are trying to live that month.

One example of the helpful commentary will show how this spirituality grows. It was the month of April, 1985, and the text was Acts 4:32, the Word of Life for the month:

> *'Now the company of those who believed were one of heart and soul, and no one said that any of the things which he possessed was his own, but they had everything in common.'*

While reading these words we might begin to think that everything worked perfectly in the community.

In fact it is Luke himself who points out that there are incidents where members of the Church of Jerusalem fail to live up to this standard (Chap. 6). However, despite these failures which are understandable, the tone of the community was set by this effort, which animated everyone, to achieve the Christian community. It is this effort which Luke wants to emphasise. The examples of those Christians who sold their property, show the revolutionary power of the Gospel, i.e. its capacity for creating totally new social relationships, with concrete effects also on the economic level.

Nobody was forced to dispose of their goods. Luke wants to show us how the Gospel, while respecting each person's freedom is able to make us overcome all the barriers that divide us, and of these barriers the selfish use of private property is one of the most serious causes of division.

'Now the company of those who believed were of one heart and soul, and no one said that any of the things which he possessed was his own, but they had everything in common.'

Naturally this social revolution starts from an inner power, from faith in and love for Jesus. For Luke this practical sharing is the unit of measurement for meaningful authentic Christian love.

No matter what economic system the Christian finds himself in, with the power of this love he will be called first and foremost to overcome every form of attachment to earthly goods, in which fear, greed and selfishness continually tend to imprison him.

'Now the company of those who believed were of one heart and soul, and no one said that any of the things which he possessed was his own, but they had everything in common.'

The examination of conscience which these words invite us to covers a very wide field of values. We need to review our relations with the political community in all that concerns our duties as citizens who are called to contribute to the common good as a sign of solidarity by paying taxes. We need to review our relations with the social community by committing ourselves in a responsible way to the building of a more just society. We need to review our relations with the church community, by giving our spare time, energy and material goods in order to help our brothers and sisters who are in need. We need to review our relations with our neighbours whose difficulties are known perhaps to us alone.

In the first community in Jerusalem, no one said that any of the things which he possessed was his own. This is the heart of the problem. What we must ascertain is whether we feel we are absolute owners or feel we are children of God and brothers and sisters in Christ who act as administrators of the goods they receive and keep others always in mind.

In the first centuries, love for Jesus, by inspiring consciences, transformed pagan society, opening it out to the progressive liberation of long-standing situations of institutionalised injustice (slavery, the exclusion of women from society, poverty, the position of the defenceless and of children in society, etc.). Why should our love for Jesus not do as much again today in the face of the serious situations of injustice in the world? Chiara Lubich.

That was enough for one month, but it continues month after month. More recently, the Word of Life for February 1993 was Matthew 5:29:

'If your right eye causes your downfall, tear it out . . .'

This seemingly absurd expression, typical of Jesus'
style, focusses our attention on an aspect of the
radical demands of the Gospel, an essential condition
for belonging to the Kingdom proclaimed by Jesus:
courage and determination in the struggle against
sin. It is an unwavering and thoroughgoing love
of good which rejects any complicity with evil and
which, as a consequence, asks the disciple to be ready
to do without even those things which are most dear
and precious when they become an occasion of sin,
an obstacle on the spiritual journey.

*'If your right eye causes your downfall, tear it
out . . .'*

This verse should be read in conjunction with the two
preceding verses (Matt. 5:27–28) where Jesus says
that 'sin' is not just an external act, but is first and
foremost an internal act: the desire to commit sin is
already sin. Now, in completing this thought, Jesus
affirms that even to put oneself deliberately in the
occasion of sin is already sin.

   Sin does not come from things, nor from outside
of us, but derives from deep within us, from our
heart. Nevertheless, precisely because we are so
vulnerable, in certain situations other people can
provoke and release in us disordered passions, so
becoming a cause of our downfall.

*'If your right eye causes your downfall, tear it
out . . .'*

We are not able to uproot the disordered passions
from our hearts; this is an arduous task which only
God can accomplish by the power of his grace. But
there is something we can do; we can show all our
good will by avoiding or removing the occasions
which can give rise to these disordered passions.
Now this is exactly what Jesus expects from us,

and he assures us that he will certainly do his part if we know how to do ours.

'If your right eye causes your downfall, tear it out . . .'

How shall we live the Word of Life this month?

First of all we should welcome with faith the teaching Jesus wants to give us. Then, going on to action, we should energetically reject all that might be an occasion of downfall for us. Let's try in particular to live this Word of Life in those moments that here Jesus seems to be referring to especially through his use of the image of the eye. One thinks of all the ways and circumstances (press, television, pictures, dress etc.) in which our looking at things and our imagination can feed a wrongful desire and so lead us into sin.

If we know how to mortify our sight externally, our inner sight will become purer, more limpid and transparent. We will see the world, people and things with new eyes, in the light and inner freedom which is Jesus's own. 'When your eye is sound,' Jesus also said, 'your whole body is full of light.' (Luke 11:34)
Chiara Lubich

This monthly Word of Life helps to unify the movement and give guidance for Christian behaviour in the world.

CHAPTER FIVE

CATCHING FIRE IN SICILY

T he heartland of the Focolare Movement is in Italy: its founder Chiara was born in Trent; its co-founder, Igino Giordani, in Tivoli; all its early pioneers were Italian. The Italian language pervades the thinking of the movement. Although a 'spirituality' has universal meaning – and the Focolare spirituality has proved its readiness to adapt to many quite different cultures – there is no doubt that language affects the expression of ideas. The various headquarters of its 'new' movements are almost all within twenty miles of Rome and its principal publishing house is in Rome. This Italian and Catholic expression is seen in the attitude to the Pope, who holds a place of honour and affection in the hearts of all its members, whether he be Pope John XXIII, Paul VI or John-Paul II. This is also part of its emphasis that the 'magisterium' of the Church is respected wholeheartedly. The same respect is encouraged in those members who belong to other churches. Members are not encouraged to move from one tradition to another, but to bring life to their own tradition. This being said, Italy remains the heartland of the movement.

It was therefore necessary to go to Italy again before proceeding further with this book and see what is happening there to the Focolare Movement in 1992 and assess the changes since first I went to research the biography, *Chiara*, in 1977 and later for *Igino Giordani*, in the 1980s.[1]

For the purposes of administration, Italy is divided into zones and I asked which I should choose for study.

Dimitri who has been my guide in all my writings about the Focolare Movement said at once, 'You should go to Sicily'. That meant the southern zone, including Sicily, Calabria and Malta. A troubled zone; Giovani Falcone, the principal investigating magistrate in Palermo, who was determined to convict the Mafia, was assassinated two days before we left for Sicily. What is happening to Chiara's 'little flock' there? My wife and I went in May-June 1992 and the movement was generous in its hospitality, giving us every opportunity to study what was relevant to the spirituality of the movement in the region. We did not go to Malta, but confined our visit to Sicily and Calabria.

The Administration

The core of the movement lies in the 'focolare', such as we have seen in London. There are eleven in the zone; two in Malta (one of men, another of women), seven in Sicily (three of men, four of women), two in Calabria (one of men, one of women). Two of those in Sicily are centres which co-ordinate the whole life of the movement; and one is a 'Mariapolis' centre. These centres have administrative duties and in them there are those who sometimes work full-time for the movement. But the word 'administration' is not quite right. Perhaps the word 'co-ordination' would be better. There is no tight control. Orders do not come from the 'centres' out to the focolare, instead experiences flow from the focolare to the centres where they are co-ordinated. Although there are responsible people in every branch of the movement, there is no hierarchy, but rather 'mutual charity'. These focolare – including the centres and the Mariapolis centre, contain some fifty people, and attached to them are sixty-five married focolarini and focolarine. In addition there are in this zone 390 volunteers. The largest element in the movement are 'the New Families'. Some of these included in the sixty-five attached to focolare as married members. In all there are 1800 couples in the 'New

Families'. This is a veritable army of people who have discovered the Focolare spirituality as a way to enrich their marriage – all have experiences to tell – and also a way to bring up the next generation of children. The vibrant nature of these 'New Families' struck me on every occasion that I met them. There are also eighty-two priests in the movement and eighty-seven (fifty-two men and thirty-five women) from the religious orders. There is happiness, joy and freedom in this 'little flock' and because of it the children and young people are at home in the movement. There is a youth organisation (the Gen) comprising about 450. About the same number of children are also involved, graded in descending ages.

My task was to assess the spirituality of the movement as I met it in each of these groups.

New Families

One of the first impressions gained of the New Families is the way in which they share their homes. The Ideal includes 'communion of goods' or 'all things in common'. This is the Church of the second century, as described by Tertullian and also in the 'Letter of Diognetus'. Hospitality is offered at once to anyone who comes to visit. One of my first experiences of this was in Catania at the home of Gaetano and Elena Veca. We were invited to a buffet supper with five couples from the New Families. The hospitality was generous, the atmosphere full of joy and ease, not rigid pietism or the semblance of a religious group. Yet, as we sat round, each told in simple terms of their debt to the movement and what it had done in their lives. As an example, let me translate the 'experience' of Elena Veca, our hostess, married with five children:

> When I look back on my life, I see it as a 'design', fashioned by God with light and shadow, but always full of his love. I was born in Calabria into a very poor family with crude, if any, morals. At four years old, I was carried off by some persons to Catania.

I did not know them, but from that day, I lost everything: mother, brothers, neighbours, house. I felt betrayed and with all the anguish within me I forgot the name of my mother, as though she had never existed. My new parents were old, without children, and they wanted the best for me, which meant keeping me healthy. I grew up among delusions and humiliations. I studied, I worked and very slowly God also began to peep into my life. I met Gaetano and we married. We wanted our family to be like that in Nazareth, but very soon we became aware that we lacked the principal component, Jesus. In 1967, we came to know the Movement – and it was a revolution. We discovered the priceless possibility of God being present among us in reciprocal love and making of our family a little church. I discovered the love of God made real for me through the love and life which Chiara had given me. Living the Ideal day by day I try to confront the sad experience of my childhood with the most profound spiritual maternity of Chiara. With this Ideal, God became my mother and the movement my true family. I discovered my place as a daughter of God and my way as giving more and more of myself because the ideal of unity flooded everything. I found a means of service through the New Family Movement. Finally, an experience enabled me to touch the beauty and the power of being one with Jesus in his will and being one with others 'that the world may believe'.

Towards the beginning of March, I noted something which was not right with my health. After examinations and X-ray, it was decided that I had a malignant growth. As I came out of the surgery, I could utter only two words '*Sia fatta*' ('that's it'). I said to Gaetano, 'Yes, this is the will of God, I accept it with all my heart and then such peace arises in my soul'. From that moment, the family competed with each other to recognise the love of God in the face of sorrow. I felt with clarity that my mode of life must now be to live every moment in the best way to give myself to the family and to others. To this end, I took time to telephone my neighbours and invited them to a meeting in the house, to express the love of this new mode of life. Between visits to the doctor and attention to the telephone for inviting the neighbours and those times when we met together as a family, there were also for me true moments of God. The words that I found within me to answer my sorrow and the suspense that I lived through, fashioned a new unity with everybody. All were happy.

On 16th March, as clearly as I can remember, my surgeon visited me and showed some surprise, but with great gentleness told me that what he had treated as a malignant growth was indeed a cancer and that he must operate at once. I felt in that moment as if he had said to me, 'Signora, you will die', or 'there is nothing more that we can do for you', which amounts to the same thing. What came to me then was that I must continue to love and be happy. At home, I talked about it with Gaetano and all the children. We felt that in the midst of us was Jesus and everyone received the news with much serenity. The day that I was to go into hospital the telephone never ceased to ring. It was the members of the Movement who wanted to assure me of their unity. I felt covered with love and tried to be 'of one heart and one mind'.

On the days that followed and all the days of waiting, a member of the New Families brought the most gracious gift to me: Jesus, the Eucharist. It was a testimony to the whole ward. On the afternoon of the 19th, the operation. I was continually of a great peace. I felt that I was resting in the arms of God and part of a great family and from my heart rose such a gratitude to Chiara, that she had shown me how to love the pain, to transform it into love. I offered my life for her for her health, for the Movement, and that all may be one. As I awoke I had much pain in my arm. I wanted to cry out, but a voice within me said repeatedly that I must look to Jesus. My relationship with Gaetano was now so much more pure, more beautiful and we had everything in common, prayer and rejoicings. When some of the children came to see me, I told them of my experience, of my discoveries. I felt that it was not enough to 'be', but that I must also speak, communicate to every person I met, the beautiful things that God had caused me to live through. The other patients and the doctors were surprised at my serenity; they marvelled at the flowers that invaded the room, at the delicate and gentle love of those who came to visit me. One nurse, worried and tense, came to me and opened her heart to me, telling of her worrisome life and she gradually recovered her smile.

When I returned home, I looked in the mirror and thought that all my dresses would just hang on me . . . I said to myself, 'What does that matter! The important thing is that your soul does not fall off you!' The soul fits point by point to the will of God. The important thing is not to have, not even to have health or an efficient body, but to be, to exist, to love. I began the therapy and I felt myself in the hands of God, wrapped in his love. Life continues with more responsibility and more coherence.

That evening in Catania, I heard of many such experiences. All were different, but all came to the same conclusion. Chiara's influence was rather like that of St Francis to the first Franciscans and John Wesley to the first Methodists. But there was a difference. The core of her influence is the inspiration to love, even pain, and to be in unity with all. This unity is attained through love and based upon the promise of Jesus that 'where two or three are gathered together in my name, there am I in the midst' (Matt 18:20). This presence of Jesus is not only in gentle benevolence and support it is also as Jesus Forsaken, i.e., abandoned by God on the cross. This last element, Jesus present as 'Jesus Forsaken' was illustrated often in Sicily.

The Courage of a Magistrate in Mafia Country

A young magistrate in Palmi met us with a group of volunteers and Gen in Reggio Calabria. She described herself as a Gen and she looked young enough. I was surprised to find that she was a magistrate in so dangerous an area, Palmi, in the region of Aspromonte in Calabria, a place of high concentration of Mafia influence. Elena Massucco is 30 years old, trained in the University of Turin. When she chose to exercise her profession as a magistrate in so dangerous an area it was not, as she said, 'a particular quality of heroism nor a desire to commit "suicide"'. It was because during her years at university she had met the Focolare Movement and participated in 'living the Ideal'. Quite simply she said, 'When I was asked if I would accept a transfer to that area, I understood that Jesus would accompany me there, present even more than in any other part.' After serving two months with an armed escort she looked at her situation. It would have been easy to be transferred to a safer place, but she considered the people who every day were guarding her and risking their lives for her. Hence she could not choose to leave if she was to remain faithful to the Gospel. Her task is not easy and she gave me a few examples of how she had to make difficult and dangerous decisions:

> During a trial, some lawyers, thinking me un-prepared, raised some exceptional difficulties with the intention of getting the case reviewed when it should have been judged. Retiring alone to my chamber, I spent a moment in prayer, asking 'counsel' from Him who alone could give it to me. I had only a quarter of an hour and hence it was impossible

for me to consult the legal texts or colleagues. I had only a sheet of paper, but wrote in peace, knowing the source of what had come to me. It was only later that I knew that the solution that I had written down coincided with what the Supreme Court had reached after years of study!

She had many such stories to tell of her trust in the Jesus who accompanied her – even when her actions were very dangerous indeed. On another occasion she told of an interrogation which she had to undertake of an accused prisoner who confessed to murders and assassinations. The hours passed and someone offered to bring her something to eat. She asked the person she was interrogating if he too would like something to eat. She added, 'In spite of the misdeeds of which he was found guilty, he was for me a neighbour whom I was required to love, even in those circumstances.' She added, 'I signed the order for his arrest and despite that, some months later, I received a letter from him in prison, when he shared with me his desperation, convinced that I would understand.'

She was not naive, but fully aware of the wound that infects the social structure. She has been long enough in the area now and has tried enough cases to realise that there is 'connivance' with evil at every level. 'Many people live in fear' she said,' because an act of courage can cost them their own life.' For her part she felt it to be her duty to support them in their anguish, their fear and, 'as far as it was possible for me, to make them accept their responsibility, speaking personally with everyone'. In this way she tried to build a solidarity among the business people, the social workers and the poor, identifying herself with them. She emphasised the fact that they were not alone and that they were more secure when they acted together. And she took the same risk as they did . . .

I am conscious of having taken in hand a 'burning'

mission against unimaginable economic interests.
There was little knowledge of right and wrong
around me. But I could not let it go on. 'Someone'
in the midst of us guided me to work for the truth. I
trust that measures will be taken that will perhaps
explode into a 'national case', and help me to find in
peace and freedom the liberty which only the 'Word'
can give. I have nothing to lose, nor is it important to
me if my career is prejudiced. It is not possible for me
to sink to compromise at all, even with my immediate
superiors; their appreciation of me sometimes goes
beyond the professional level but they find it difficult
to maintain a calm dialogue with me. I speak to them
of my choice to live the Gospel first and my wish to
act according to its logic and re-examine my position
in relation to it in everything.

In this she has demonstrated the courage of a deep
conviction and illustrated for me the cost of living the
Ideal in practical terms and with integrity.

Solidarity in a Housing Estate

Gela on the south coast of Sicily was once one of the
pleasantest places on the island. Lawrence Durrell, who
deplored its present state, writes, 'Even in the mess of
modern Gela one sees how sweet a place it must have
been, how rich in fruit and vine and how splendid as
horse country because so well watered and green.' It
escaped invasions because it lay back from the sea, but it
suffered first from an oil refinery and now the fertile land
is destroyed by the exploitation of builders who control
the town. Only one hotel is allowed in this place which
has much history to attract tourists. One could say that
almost the whole economy is controlled by the Mafia. I was
taken first to see the ravaged fields, now housing people
in slum conditions. Not a child or an adult could be seen
on the street. Notices warned us that it was dangerous
to drive through the estates. In few of them were there
any public utilities. Rocco who showed me round was a

volunteer in the Focolare Movement and, with his wife, Rosa, they constitute a strong 'New Family'. Rocco and his family moved into a housing estate on the other side of the town, where conditions were bad. Rocco then roused the tenants to do something for themselves. He showed his love towards the neighbours in a very practical way. There is nothing sentimental about him or his wife, yet faithfully they seek to live the Ideal: to love into unity, to recognise that with Jesus in the midst all things are possible, and to accept the consequences of challenging evil, as Jesus did on the cross. They began to change the face of their estate, enlisting the help of 500 local residents, forming a residents association which then attracted finance from the local government. The difference between his estate and that which I had first seen is astonishing. The houses are not luxury dwellings, but ordinary workers' dwellings. They are clean and well appointed, the streets are safe, they are laying out an attractive piazza. Children play happily in the streets. Several neighbours came in to see me when I was in Rocco and Rosa's flat and also some members of the movement. We talked and it was clear that the Focolare movement had acted as an antidote to the Mafia, inspired by the strength of love and unity. Rocco is a policeman and his wife an active participant in the social services of the area. They both demonstrate the practical nature of the Ideal when it is lived in dangerous and difficult situations.

Focolare Priests

We met only two priests. The movement is a lay movement, but it is evident that priests who find their way to it, find new life in their priesthood and true happiness. Living the Ideal, especially in consideration of 'Jesus Forsaken', often means accepting, even choosing, particularly difficult parishes, but the support of the movement and the sense of new life in the vocation of priesthood is more than compensation for a difficult parish!

Father Pietro in Noto is a prison chaplain, with what he calls a 'life sentence', and there cannot be a prisoner in that prison who does not hope that he is in, if not for his life, at least for the term of their own sentences. I could interview only two prisoners, but they both saw Father Pietro as their true 'father', not only in the spiritual sense. They both depended upon him in and out of prison. One seemed to me to have an inordinately long sentence for his unwilling involvement in an armed robbery. Father Pietro had sustained him in building up a little business in the town and arranged for him to serve the remaining years of his sentence in prison at night and at his work by day. He had not made him a very religious man, but he had enabled him to live a life of human dignity. In fact, he had loved him and cared for him until there was a bond of unity between them which made the presence of Jesus real to a man who found little in the church to interest him.

The second prisoner was one whom it must have been very difficult to love. His record was, in human terms, despicable. Father Pietro saw a brother in him and had more than once enabled him to make a fresh start. He had let him down each time, but Father Pietro persisted. He spent money and time and care on one whom most people would have thought not worth it. The change taking place in him, however, is noticeable. You cannot forever resist the squadrons of love. There is nothing naive about Father Pietro, but there is a persistence, which in this priest is based upon the presence of Jesus in the midst. He is attached to the Central Focolare in Catania and makes the journey from Noto every week and cooks for them. It is not the service, but the fellowship that keeps him satisfied, although the service too gladdens his heart and theirs.

The other priest I met was Don Franco, who was a parish priest in Palermo. He had been a priest since 1964 and was appointed parish priest in his native Palermo in 1968 at the age of 27. He had only been in his own parish for about a year when he was invited to a Mariapolis, or rather to take a group of young people there. He did not expect to gain anything from the Mariapolis for himself, but thought it might be good for the young people, who did not have much chance to get out into the country for a holiday. He discovered that there were other priests there who formed a close fellowship to which he was readily admitted. His experience of priests so far was that they were loners, caring for their own parishes, but not bothering too much about other priests. These seemed to care for him. When he returned to Palermo, he looked at his fellow-priests with different eyes. He went again to a meeting of about thirty priests in Reggio Calabria and the wonder persisted.

Then something happened that changed his life. It was quite simple. Three priests from Syracuse, which in those days before the motorway was four hours journey from him, came to spend an hour with him. It was not what they said, but that they drove for eight hours on the road to care for him which impressed him. He knew then that he had to go to the Focolare centre personally and without invitation to give himself up. The love of the movement had captured him. In 1972, he became a Focolare priest. He has remained in Palermo, although changed his parish, always on request from his bishop to do a specific and difficult job. Now every Tuesday, five Focolare priests come together in unity and help one another to live the Ideal. This unity among priests has been a great joy to him as to others. When he was first ordained to the priesthood and had soon acquired his own parish, he thought of himself as the teacher, if not the master, but now he saw that the world had greater need of witnesses than of teachers or masters. He lived among his people and the love and care he showed was his most eloquent teaching. It changed also his attitude to his bishop whose authority he had sometimes resented. In good Focolare fashion he read the words of Jesus, 'He who hears you, hears me' as an authority of Jesus given to the bishop by apostolic succession.

When he had been ten years in his first parish, the

bishop asked him to go to a very run-down parish which
had suffered from an elderly priest who had not been
able to do more than read the services. Although there
had been four priests in that parish, all fairly elderly,
the senior priest had engendered a sense of lethargy.
Don Franco came as leader of the parish, although the
youngest among the four priests. He saw at once the
meaning of the Ideal, putting Jesus in the midst and
built a rich fellowship among the priests. For six years
the parish grew and he was happy. Then the bishop sent
him to a parish which had suffered from many problems
and where respect for the priesthood was low. He went
there in 1984 and saw the need to build unity. He
succeeded and for seven years he enjoyed his growing
unity with the people. He was sorry to leave it, but the
bishop transferred him in 1991 to the most difficult parish
that anyone could imagine. The area is very poor, beset
with many special problems, high illiteracy and youth
delinquency. There is exploitation of youth, family life
has all but collapsed, prostitution, drug addiction, and
violence is evident. All this on a large scale. All he and
his helpers can do is deal with people one by one. Children
from six to thirteen are picked up off the streets and,
with the help of a dedicated nun, who has also felt the
influence of the movement, the children are taught and
cared for. Seven families have been brought under the
influence of the movement and there is a branch of the
Gen, with four members.

I do not lack difficulties in my personal life, (said
Don Franco) and in the parish community; but the
love of Jesus Forsaken is the key which solves every
problem, because of the certainty of the resurrection.
It is thus that I try to help, as I did recently when
a child was killed and a father, like the driver of
the magistrate Giovanni Falcone, who was involved
in such a horrible assassination, on the eve of his
daughter's first communion. I visited the father in
hospital and despite his grave condition, I was able

to speak with him. Although in great distress and seriously ill, he was glad to know that the whole parish was with him and prayed for his recovery.

For me, it was the experience of seeing in the darkness of such a meaningless act, the light shining through, with the certainty that God was manifesting himself as love in a situation which humanly speaking was unbearable. I was assured that notwithstanding this and similar terrible acts, the Risen One was present and making a new heaven and a new earth.

A Focolare Household in Calabria

Guido and Lucia, with their three children live in a house in Locri, which is specially designed to accommodate all kinds of Focolare activities. It is on four levels with a multitude of rooms, all well equipped for meetings of different kinds. On any evening it hums from top to bottom. The Gen are in the basement, self-contained and disturbing no one, but very lively and with music that means a great deal to young people. On another floor there is a meeting for engaged couples preparing for their marriage. Some members of the movement came to see me in another room. My group kept growing – a Muslim from Senegal, the head of the Gynaecological Department at the hospital where Guido is a doctor, a solicitor, a local government officer, a baker, a sales representative, a teacher, a shopkeeper, a social worker, and a housewife. All had stories to tell of how the movement had enabled them to live and work as disciples of Jesus Christ. The experiences all told of caring for people, of discovering the power of Jesus in the midst of suffering, which then glowed with light and led to a deeper sense of the presence of Jesus. There was little that was pietistic or sentimental. All their stories were practical stories of work done and of lives lived according to the Ideal in difficult circumstances. They spoke of faith restored when they came together. And so much else that told

of a vibrant movement. They were not given to religious
demonstration although each was regular in receiving the
body of Christ at the Eucharist. There was no ostentation
about their religion.

My attention went soon to the Senegalese, Kandii whom
I discovered was not the only Senegalese who found his
home in the house of Guido and Lucia. Senegal is a
poor country with a growing population. It was under
French rule for about three hundred years, becoming
independent in 1960. Unemployment has grown steadily
over the years and many young men have left for France
and other countries with coasts on the Mediterranean.
Italy was a natural choice for many, as it was for the
youth of Morocco. In Calabria it was mostly Senegalese.
Lucia seems to have met them first and her reaction to
them is typical of the movement when confronted with
young people in need:

> It was in the street market that I met them one day
> and noticed several young immigrant boys living on
> the street. There was a little push from my maternal
> instinct which made me think of what difficulties
> these young men must encounter, so far from home,
> in a strange country, with the colour of their skin
> adding to their difficulties. I knew that they came
> from Senegal or Morocco and asked myself: 'these
> boys come to the market to earn their living, but
> then what do they do? God knows what dangers they
> encounter as they go around ... What alternative
> have they?'

She made a point of going to the market, accompanied
later by Guido, every Friday and bought and exchanged
necessary things with them, although they spoke little
Italian. They were invited home and taught the language,
but most of all, given a home where they could call
at any time. Guido and Lucia offered them care and
love. They dealt with their problems. Although they
were all Muslims, there seemed to be no difficulty in

understanding one another's religion. Jesus could be in the midst also when Christian and Muslim were together. Guido and Lucia with their home and children have provided a basis for all the drama of their life. They have celebrated Christmas together, they have united families in Italy, and enabled Senegalese to integrate into Italian life.

The Testimony of a Mussulman

One of the Senegalese when asked about the reaction of Muslims to this approach by Christians, said with evident sincerity:

> We are all Mussulmen and this rapport with the Christians of Locri and with their experience of the Gospel has shown to us, many of us, a new dimension in our own religion and how to live it much more seriously . . . I have seen a people who have more faith than we have, who love, asking nothing in return, who consider all men their brothers . . . As for us, who are often suspicious of foreigners and also indifferent to one another, this contrast is a strong testimony inviting us to change. For example, for the first time we have now helped a man recently arrived from Senegal with his wife, who was wounded in a street incident. At a gathering when we were all together, we spoke about this man saying to the other Senegalese: 'See how unfortunate is this brother who cannot work to support his family.' We then collected many things among ourselves, because we are able, and have given them to him. This is the first time this has happened.

Aliune, who said that, has become a metal worker and obtained a good position. In Senegal, he has four brothers whom he helps with regular contributions. Lucia was particularly concerned about how the separate families lived and asked him as well as some Senegalese women,

how they managed. She and Guido began to work for
the reunion of families in Italy. It was obvious that men
separated from their wives put a great strain on family
life. They have now succeeded in bringing many wives
over to join their husbands and complete their families.

'This recomposition of the family,' Guido commented,
'has a beneficial social effect, not only on the country from
which they come but also upon the host country.' Aliune
expressed a ready agreement to this.

The Witness of a Forester in Aspromonte

When we were taken from Locri across Aspromonte to
Reggio Calabria to see a mixed group of people influenced
by the Focolare Movement, I met first of all a man who
had responsibility for protecting the forest in a dangerous
part of that district. In this area the power of the Mafia
is very great and it is very difficult to enforce the law.
Enzo Bagnato loves the forest and both professionally
and personally he wishes to see it preserved. He has
been threatened and is naturally concerned about his
wife and four children, but he continues with his work,
as little able to compromise in his field as Elena Massucco
is in her legal profession. He is like her in many ways.
He too was offered a safer job in Bologna and, for the
sake of his family, he was tempted to accept. In the
week he had to decide, there came into his office all
those who had worked with him in defence of the forest:
colleagues, forest guards, workers, apprentices, students
working on their theses. They were bewildered, deluded,
without hope. 'I could not let them down,' he said. He is
a volunteer in the movement and when he considered his
commitment to live the Ideal, he saw clearly that that
meant loving all those who were dependent upon him in
his work. He saw that it was his task to 'reinstate' the
presence of God where he worked. He had fought quite a
fight against those who wished to destroy his forest and
he had to ask the question afresh, 'Can I give up now?'
Despite all the obvious advantages of the transfer, with

the higher salary and better conditions for the family, greater prospects in his career, etc, he could not go. After the decision, he said: 'I give glory to God that, thanks to Chiara, he has made me understand that my place is with my people who seek more dignity, more justice, more love, more credibility in the institution.'

An American Methodist in the Focolare Movement

Towards the end of our visit to Sicily, I met an American Methodist minister from Wisconsin, with whom I talked frankly about his links with the Focolare Movement. He lives with his Italian wife and family in Scicli, a beautiful town not far from the southern coast of Sicily. In Scicli there is a Waldensian community as well as a small Baptist church and his Methodist church. The majority of people in Scicli, as in any part of Sicily, are Catholics. He works very closely with the movement and I asked him whether the Focolare Movement is not locked into the structure of the Roman Catholic Church. Was there any possibility of it making progress in other church traditions to any great extent? Individuals, of course, because there is much purely Christian attraction about the beliefs and practices of its members that must appeal to all. What about worship together? He told me how his joint work with the Waldensians had in no way prevented Catholics and Protestants attending one another's services. Social work they had done jointly and several focolarini had worshipped with him, while he had worshipped happily in the Catholic Church.

The Revd. John Hobbins came to Italy to study some ten years ago and, although a Methodist, he did not choose Germany or Scandinavia to study, but Rome. He wanted to study the life of the early Church and he had met a Jesuit scholar in America with whom he could study in Rome. He came to Europe. At first, the Catholic Church as he met it in Brussels seemed moribund. Then in Rome, he was not much impressed by its spiritual power. It seemed, he said, more interested in secular power. Even the fellow students at the Pontifical University (Gregoriana) who had been sent by their bishops, seemed more interested in power games in the Church and they made a poor impression on him. He was much more impressed by the students who had come from India and Mexico, because they had spiritual ideals. He was disappointed. Then he came to Scicli in 1989 to be the pastor of a Methodist church. It was there that he met the Focolare Movement. When I spoke to him he had been there two and a half years and his contact with the movement had quite changed his ideas about Catholics. They seemed to him to possess humility to an unusual degree. They took no steps to advertise what they were doing – and he soon discovered that they were doing a great deal. Their emphasis was giving, caring for people and creating unity by their love. It was, of course, from them that he heard about Chiara Lubich, a charismatic leader. There was, he thought, a measure of hero worship in the movement, but as he read what she wrote, he realised that she had a great deal to say to the Church, Catholic and Protestant. Within the Catholic context, Chiara has a natural authority, helping, advising, loving and caring, rather than imposing her ideas.

It was, for me, a very great help to talk with a Protestant minister who had spent two and a half years working with the Focolare Movement in Catholic Sicily. He recognised the difficulty of attracting Protestants into a primarily Catholic movement, but while admitting that the majority of its members were Catholic, he saw real hope for ecumenical advance. The respect for one's own spiritual leaders is a great help. The Focolare Movement does not attempt to proselytise. That is not their way. Those who come from other traditions find that the movement encourages them to take their own tradition more seriously. John Hobbins saw that the movement might be imitated in other traditions and develop in parallel, but hoped that that would not happen. The essence of the movement is unity and once Protestants become attracted to it they should be able to develop within the whole movement. There are already examples of united development which has avoided such parallel movements. The Orthodox Church, for example, in Greece and Eastern Europe have practically no experience of united work with Roman Catholics. Yet, Chiara quite early developed a relationship with these churches which did not lead to separate development. Again, in Bavaria, at Ottmaring, Catholics and Lutherans grow together in unity and love.

John Hobbins thought that the movement should be more courageous in its ecumenical work. While I was in Sicily there was much talk of the Catholic missions to Scandinavia, particularly Sweden. John, who is of Swedish origin, approved of this. He thought that alternative churches helped all to grow. He brought the open American mind to the relationship between different denominations and was prepared to defend competition. No denomination should consider that a particular part of the world belonged to it. He even welcomed competition. He was also prepared to say that his experiences had shown that the Methodists, Waldensians and Baptists in Italy had done the Catholic Church a lot of good, by just being there and forcing the 'established' Church to examine its own work. There is need for a maturity in ecumenical work which should by now have outgrown the adolescent period of the World Council of Churches. He was convinced that the Focolare Movement had achieved this and was the key to a slow, but organic union of the churches. The method is not by negotiation, but by living and loving the world side by side, in competition if necessary. There was no doubt in my mind that he had learned greatly from Chiara and admired the amount she had already achieved among the other churches and other religions.

The members of the movement have an extraordinary freedom. Although many are devout Catholics they are prepared to criticise some actions of their own Church. Not all of them, for example, support the political party

most favoured by the Church. Some have given their
support to new parties which stand for principles, rather
than political programmes.

After this long conversation with John Hobbins I realise
how much the movement has to offer in renewing the
spiritual life of all the churches. He had seen it as I had –
as striving to live the Ideal, accepting Christ's command
to 'love one another' as a way of life, experiencing the
power of Jesus in the midst and being prepared to suffer
with Jesus who was forsaken on the cross.

CHAPTER SIX

JESUS FORSAKEN

At the centre of the Focolare Movement is the person of Jesus. This is at first most evident in the unifying power of Jesus when 'two or three are met together in his name'. That is the daily experience of all focolarini, twenty-four hours out of every twenty-four hours! As they face a problem they meet together and claim the promise that Jesus be in the midst of them. I have even heard some say, 'Let us put Jesus in the midst' – slightly heretical, but so living is this experience of 'Jesus in the midst', that the phrase is excusable. And if Jesus is in the midst no problem is insoluble. Indeed, there have been enough examples in this book already of unbelievable achievements with Jesus in the midst. There was Rocca and Rosa in Sicily, for example, and the experiences of those young people in London.

This sense of power, however, needs correction. There is nothing triumphalist about the Focolare Movement. People fail, they suffer and indeed choose suffering when it seems to be God's will and his way. 'Jesus in the midst' can be the young Jesus of Nazareth, silencing his critics, healing the sick, cleansing the lepers and even raising the dead. There seems no limit to his power. But it can also be Jesus on the cross, dying and forsaken. The words 'My God, my God, why hast thou forsaken me?', are also the words of that same Jesus. From this discovery has come a very important part of the Focolare spirituality. It was illustrated by Elena Veca in Catania, who faced cancer with the conviction that God required it of her. She saw the union with God through Jesus as requiring

suffering and even being abandoned. Jesus had so warned
his disciples:

> 'Blessed are you when people insult you, persecute
> you and falsely say all kinds of evil against you
> because of me', (Matt. 5:11, NIV) and even, 'Then
> you will be handed over to be persecuted and put
> to death, and you will be hated.' (Matt. 24:9 NIV).
> And the warning against popularity is even clearer,
> 'Woe to you when all men speak well of you.' (Luke
> 6:26 NIV)

There are other such texts in the Gospels, enough to warn
Christians that they are not to expect a carefree life,
always protected by an almighty God who treats them
like an indulgent mother.

You cannot take Jesus without the cross and however
bejewelled you make the cross, his cry will not be silenced.
'My God, my God, why hast thou forsaken me?' That cry
of dereliction is not explained as only the first verse of
Psalm 22, which ends in triumph. At least not in the
experience of Jesus, who had already faced its awful
darkness in Gethsemane. But for us, the cross leads to
the resurrection. We, therefore, suffer and sorrow, but
not without hope. Elena's words go to the heart of it:
'From my heart rose such a gratitude to Chiara, that
she had taught me to love the pain.'

Dietrich Bonhoeffer

There are many points at which Lutheran and Catholic
spirituality meet. Bonhoeffer who was through and
through a Lutheran, discovered for himself the meaning
of 'Jesus Forsaken'. He did not put it in that way, but
he turned away from triumphalism or any sense that
the almighty God would come to his faithful servant and
rescue him from all ills. Like Karl Barth before him, he
rejected the idea of God as a *deus ex machina*, that
theatrical device for coming in from the wings to rescue
the actor. At a very dark hour in the struggle against

Hitler, when he knew that an attempt was about to be made on Hitler's life, he wrote a poem which contrasted the Christian with the pagan:

> Men go to God when they are sore bestead,
> Pray to him for succour, for his peace, for bread,
> For mercy for them sick, sinning or dead;
> All men do so Christian and unbelieving.
>
> Men go to God when he is sore bestead,
> Find him poor and scorned, without shelter
>   or bread,
> Whelmed under weight of the wicked, the weak,
>   the dead;
> Christians stand by God in his hour of grieving.
>
> God goes to every man when sore bestead,
> Feeds body and spirit with his bread;
> For Christians, pagans alike he hangs dead,
> And both alike forgiving.

In a covering letter which he sent with that poem from prison to his friend Eberhard Bethge, he pointed out its meaning:

> The poem about Christians and pagans contains an idea that you will recognize: 'Christians stand by God in his hour of grieving'; that is what distinguishes Christians from pagans. Jesus asked in Gethsemane, 'Could you not watch with me one hour?' That is a reversal of what the religious man expects from God. Man is summoned to share in God's suffering at the hands of a godless world. He must therefore really live in the godless world, without attempting to gloss over or explain its ungodliness in some religious way or other. He must live a 'secular' life, and thereby share in God's suffering. He *may* live a secular life (as one who has been freed from false religious obligations and inhibitions). To be a Christian does not mean to

be religious in a particular way, to make something
of oneself (a sinner, a penitent or a saint) on the
basis of some method or other, but to be a man –
not a type of man, but the man that Christ creates
in us. It is not the religious act that makes the
Christian, but participation in the sufferings of God
in the secular.

He goes on to say that the specific Christian attitude is
not in the first place thinking about one's own needs,
problems, sins and fears, but allowing oneself to be
caught up into the way of Jesus Christ, into what he
calls 'the messianic event' (July 18, 1944).[1]

Only two days earlier, he had been wrestling with what
participation in the powerlessness of God in the world
means for a Christian. He is not sure of his argument,
but is convinced that he has touched upon something
true. He has been trying on that day to think of God in
a non-religious way and also developing his thesis of the
'world come of age', no longer in tutelage to the Church,
but free and responsible before God. He adds:

When we speak of God in a non-religious way, we
must speak of him in such a way that the godlessness
of the world is not in some way concealed, but rather
revealed, and thus exposed to an unexpected light.
The world that has come of age is more godless, and
perhaps for that very reason nearer to God, than the
world before the coming of age.

Bonhoeffer himself admitted that he was putting things
clumsily and longed to meet with his friend and discuss
it all. He saw the value of meeting together when the
presence of Jesus in the midst would clarify much that
was obscure.

In this earlier letter he had come nearer to Chiara's
understanding of 'Jesus Forsaken':

The God who is with us is the God who forsakes us.

The God who lets us live in the world without the working hypothesis of God is the God before whom we stand continually. Before God and with God we live without God. God lets himself be pushed out of the world on to a cross. He is weak and powerless in the world, and that is precisely the way, the only way, in which he is with us and helps us. (This was to fulfil what was spoken by the prophet Isaiah, 'He took our infirmities and bore our diseases'. Matt. 8:17) Christ helps us, not by virtue of his omnipotence, but by virtue of his weakness and suffering. The Bible directs attention to God's powerlessness and suffering; only the suffering God can help.

Bonhoeffer was disillusioned with his church because it had chosen the easy way of fighting to preserve itself instead of witnessing to the suffering of God in and for the world. His experiences were quite different from those of Chiara, but they both came within sight of a revelation that God is with us in our suffering, not to remove it but to use it. It was because the churches in Germany had failed to accept the suffering that they had failed. These letters of 1944 were only a few months after Chiara's recognition of 'Jesus Forsaken' as a key to her spirituality.

The Moment of Greatest Suffering

Unity and Jesus Forsaken were among the first elements in Focolare spirituality. This can be seen from the numerous letters that have been preserved from the earliest days of the movement. Chiara remembered that one of the earliest episodes of the history of this idea came in the house of Dori Zamboni, one of the first focolarine, on 24th January 1944. Dori was ill, probably due to an infection she had contracted on one of her visits to the poorest district of Trent to minister to some poor families. She was so ill that it was not wise for her to go to church to attend the mass, so Chiara asked a priest

to bring the communion to her. She was with her when
Dori received communion and Dori remembered that the
priest asked Chiara, at what point in his Passion Jesus
suffered most. She replied that she had always thought
that it was when they raised the cross. But the priest
said, 'I think, in fact, that it was that moment on the
cross when he cried out, "My God! My God! Why hast
thou forsaken me?".' Chiara turned those words over in
her mind and said, 'If the greatest sorrow that Jesus had
was to be forsaken by his Father, then we must choose
that as an ideal and follow it.'

Dori commented that in that moment she realised that
their ideal must be, in mind and imagination, fixed upon
Jesus when he turned to his Father in agony and cried
aloud to him. Then she said, 'My poor pains, seen in
the shadow of his suffering, could give me joy, because
they made me a little like him.' 'From that day', she
said, 'Chiara spoke often and continuously of "Jesus
Forsaken". This was the living *persona* of our existence.'

Looking back to those early days, Chiara asked the
question of the effect this element had in their spirituality,
particularly in association with the strong sense of Jesus
in the midst. When they spoke of unity, they saw it in
communion with others and understood it as the unity
created by Jesus, by the Risen One, who was 'felt, seen,
enjoyed'. All enjoyed his presence, all sorrowed at his
absence. He is peace, joy, love, ardour; he creates the
conditions for heroism, and generosity. And these effects
are fruits of the Spirit of Jesus, who is the Holy Spirit.
The Spirit of the risen Jesus, in our midst, forms Jesus
in us, and we appear to others to be a continuation of
his presence, the body of Christ, the Church. Whoever,
in fact, builds unity with reciprocal love, lives the death
of Christ and his resurrection. Live then, Chiara would
say, the life that never dies. Jesus said: '. . . who lives and
believes in me shall never die' (John 11:26). Although an
individual Christian can experience the same effects in
the arms of Jesus Forsaken, it must lead to unity. From
this the focolarini have concluded that the Christian

is not and never can be isolated. It has been their experience that the acceptance of Jesus Forsaken, with consequent acceptance of suffering, results in the fulness of the presence of the Risen Lord. This presence has the intensity, strength, power, that signifies he is totally with them, in full unity. It is from such experiences that questions are asked about the Church. Chiara and her companions began to seek the relationship between Jesus Crucified and Forsaken and the gift of the Holy Spirit.

Sources of Jesus Forsaken in the Gospels and the Early Fathers

'When Jesus had received the vinegar, he said, "It is finished"; and he bowed his head and gave up his spirit'. (John 19:30, RSV)

There is a comment on this verse by S. Lyonnet,

'John's expression, "gave up his spirit" is unusual. The verb to *give up* (the spirit) seems to be chosen to indicate a voluntary offering on the part of Christ, i.e. choosing to give up his life. By using such an unusual expression to indicate the death of Jesus, John wished to say that that death had the effect of giving the Spirit to the community.'[2]

This is supported by a comment in the *Traduzione Ecumenica della Bibbia*, (Ecumenical Translation of the Bible), at this point in the text: 'John wished to suggest that by means of his death, Jesus is able to transmit the Spirit to the world.' E.Y. Congar is even more precise, '. . . Jesus breathed upon Mary and John, who were like the Church at the foot of the cross, and he transmitted the Spirit.'[3]

Jerome, commenting on John 7:39, affirms: 'The Spirit was not yet given, because Jesus was not yet glorified, i.e. not yet crucified.'

Ambrose noted that

'When Christ was crucified he thirsted and was

pierced like the rock which poured out water in the
desert, and that promise of John 7:38 was fulfilled,
"in that moment when he thirsted, there poured
from his side rivers of living water to quench the
thirst of all".'

Paul said that Christ had become a curse for us by his
death on the cross, in order that we might receive the
promise of the Spirit (Gal. 3:13–14).

In the writings of Chiara there are many such quotations and in all of them she keeps closely to the text of
the New Testament and the Fathers.

They seem to point quite clearly to the conclusion
that by embracing Jesus Crucified and Forsaken, the
Holy Spirit can pour out his spiritual gifts, his fruits,
upon us, and that the Risen One can manifest himself
in everyone of us.

Jesus Forsaken as the Key to Our Unity with Others

Jesus Forsaken is not only the key to our unity of the
soul with God. He is also the key to our unity with our
neighbour. The Focolare Movement takes this theme to
be of fundamental importance. Choosing to love God is
also a choice of a life lived for love. Jesus said, 'I give you
a new commandment: that you love one another.' That
is all he desires of us. No one has ever made himself so
completely one with others as Jesus Forsaken. Because
of this the movement takes 'Jesus Forsaken' as its model
of one who loves. It is no accident that the girls in Trent
in the earliest days discovered the power of the verse,
'Greater love has no one than this: that a man lay down
his life for his friends.' In asking one another, 'Are you
ready to die for me?' they had already seen Jesus crucified
as their model. Now, it was to go to the extreme point of
suffering. It was when Jesus was forsaken of his Father
that they deepened the Focolare spirituality. This became
the key to unity with others. Like him they sought to
'make themselves one'.

But what do these three simple words mean: *make themselves one*?

In Italian it is just two words, *'Farsi uno'*.

It is not possible to enter into the soul of a brother in order to understand him or share his sorrows if our mind is preoccupied with judging him or thinking about some other matter. The *'farsi uno'* requires a poverty of spirit, 'poor in spirit'. Only in this way is unity possible. Where then, do we turn to learn this great art, to be poor in spirit, which, according to the Gospel, carries with it the kingdom of heaven, which is the kingdom of love, love in the soul? We turn to Jesus Forsaken, none is poorer than he: he, who after having lost almost all his disciples, after having given his mother away, and also given his life for us, must experience the terrible feeling of being forsaken by his own Father.

When we look to him, as Paul did, we find our model. 'To the weak I became weak, that I might win the weak. I have become all things to all men, that I might by all means save some.' (1 Cor. 9:22)

The Focolare Movement has built this into its statutes:

The life of union among the faithful ... claims from its members a very special love for the cross and in particular for Jesus in the mystery of his passion: the divine model for as many as desire to cooperate in the union of men with God and with one another, stripped of all external things and above all of interior things ...

Then the statute adds the cry of Jesus: 'My God! My God! Why hast thou forsaken me?'. 'Jesus Forsaken', then, is the origin of the unity. There is yet another way in which 'Jesus Forsaken' leads to unity. Jesus said, 'I in them and thou in me, that they may become perfectly one' (John 17:23). Jesus is then present in every Christian, making for perfect unity.

But how is it possible that Jesus can realise in us his 'I in them'? Chiara's answer to that question is:

We have spoken of Jesus Forsaken as the key to unity of the soul with God It is now necessary to embrace generously and without hesitation the One who presents himself to us in the sorrows of every day, in the renunciations of the Christian way and all the strength that that brings. Then the Risen One who hopefully is already in us by grace, radiates all his splendour; the gifts of his Spirit flow into our souls; an Easter is renewed in us every time; Jesus lives fully in every one of us. But if Jesus lives in me and lives also in my brother, it is evident that when we meet we are already one, we are perfect in unity. And what makes that possible? The love of Jesus Forsaken.

Within the movement there are many texts which emphasise this truth that Jesus Forsaken, when properly understood is the way to unity. No text is clearer than, 'I, if I be lifted up from the earth, will draw all men unto me' (John 12:32, AV). And surely this is to make all one.

The Love of Jesus Forsaken in the Various Movements

The focolarini, as well as other members of the movement, orientate their thinking towards Jesus Forsaken. This becomes clear in some of the 'new' movements which have radiated out from the centre like rays of the sun. For example, the New Family Movement successfully confronts the problems of the orphans. Bearing in mind the teaching of Matthew 25, the parable of the Last Judgement, they see the face of Jesus in the face of the orphan. The face of the orphan reflects back to them the forsaken Jesus on the cross – alone, without protection or companions. They can with imagination feel that in serving these helpless children they are serving the forsaken Christ. In Catania, I met two robust but elderly ladies who had for years held open house for unmarried mothers and pregnant prostitutes. They were not reforming them, or judging them, although some would find new ways of life through their care. They simply received them, cared for them, built them into a community, cared for their babies. This was no house of correction, nor was it a social service. It was two women who had caught the vision of Jesus Forsaken and saw his face in the faces of these young women, often mere girls themselves, and their babies. They loved them and loved Jesus Forsaken in them. The house was called, 'The House of the Family'. Others in the New Family Movement confronted the problems of separation, of divorce, of the elderly, of the generation gap, etc. in the same way. In every person in need there was a forsaken Jesus to be embraced.

Much the same applies to the New Humanity Movement, which attempts to confront the thousands of problems of humanity in the different areas of human life: work, unemployment, tensions between social classes etc.: and in politics, the problems of human rights, the rapport between parties. Many of the movement have supported political parties, because of their care for the oppressed, but seldom for their dogmatic party programmes.

These activities are not simply good deeds done in an amateurish way. They are highly professional. Where someone has felt the call to respond and does not have the qualifications, there are always opportunities for training or professionally trained advisers to consult.

The international journal of the movement, *Città Nuova* which appears fortnightly in Italian, gives evidence of the highly professional work of the movement. It also gives evidence of its wide-ranging concerns in politics, social ethics, education, the arts, literature and trends in philosophy.

A Necessary Warning and an Emphasis

Chiara has a warning lest this wide range of interests should be interpreted as a 'renewal movement', seeking a new form of society:

But the Focolare Movement – and this needs to be emphasised – is not primarily concerned with the renewal of the family, of youth or of the various areas of human life in society. Neither does it have as its principal objective to resolve the problems of the religious orders, the priests, the seminarians or the parishes . . . even though it may contribute to the resolution and renewal of all these.

The Focolare Movement has as its objective to contribute to the realisation of the Testament of Jesus in the world, and that is why its movements have so wide a range – why they look to the youth, to the family, to the parishes, to society, to the priests, to the religious orders – to create, to form a unified tapestry of the various components of the Christian world and to manifest to the world what the Church is like when Christ, the Risen One, is in the midst of his children.

It is in this way, above all, by this testimony to unity – a testimony which is the premise for every other apostolic activity – that the Movement feels the possibility to share with the Church, its actual concerns and its sorrows.[4]

The Focolare Movement has reached out to the problems of what we used to call 'The Third World', with some success, and has come into fellowship with many different traditions in the Church. Its non-dogmatic approach, the centrality of love and its single-minded objective of unity has made this possible. Not by negotiation, but by love have they conquered. Chiara insists that the bridges they have built were possible most of all because of Jesus Forsaken. The unity of Christ's suffering is more effective than an agreed text drafted at a conference.

CHAPTER SEVEN

THE EUCHARIST

L iving the Ideal means loving God and that leads to loving the world, as God loves the world (John 3:16). Chiara, with her Catholic background saw this in terms of what Mary did, i.e. 'giving Christ to the world'. How then is Christ present? Bonhoeffer, in his 'Christology' lectures in 1933, answered this question with three means of Christ's expression in the Church as part of the world: in the Word, in the sacrament and in the community. Chiara would not quarrel with that, but she finds Christ present in six ways:

1. 'Jesus in the midst' – where two or three are gathered together in his name – Bonhoeffer's 'community'.
2. 'Jesus in the Eucharist' – this is my body broken for you – Bonhoeffer's 'sacrament'.
3. 'Jesus in his word' – if you continue in my word you are truly my disciples – part of what Bonhoeffer meant by 'the Word'.
4. 'Jesus is our brother' – inasmuch as you have done it to the least of these my brothers, you have done it unto me – Bonhoeffer would have no difficulty with that.
5. 'Jesus in the hierarchy' – he who hears you hears me. Bonhoeffer would no doubt differ here, or at least need to discuss.
6. 'Jesus in me' – if I listen to the voice of the Spirit who speaks within. I am sure that Bonhoeffer would understand.

My references to Bonhoeffer are because, of all modern theologians, he is the most Lutheran. Where I have written Bonhoeffer I could have written Martin Luther.

Our immediate interest is in the second of Chiara's presences of Jesus – the Eucharist. In this, she would be very much at home with both Bonhoeffer and Martin Luther. Throughout his life Martin Luther remained committed to the Catholic doctrine of the Mass. But already in the Reformation period, the attempts to define the meaning of the Mass caused great division. Luther could never get away from the clear words of Jesus: 'This is my body', 'except you eat the flesh of the Son of Man', and many other words. Luther refused to meet Zwingli because of his different interpretation of the Mass. We have a sorry history of quarrelling about the meaning of the Eucharist, but all who long for true unity know that it cannot be assumed until we receive together at the same table. On that day, there may be many explanations going through our minds, but they will be lost in the wonder of our obedience to the Lord's command and our adoration of his presence with us. For this reason, I do not intend to try to reconcile the various interpretations, but simply to describe what the Eucharist means to those who live the Ideal.

The Early Experiences

When Chiara was still a young school teacher in Castello, many people remarked upon her frequent 'communions'. She 'adored the tabernacle', they said. For a Catholic, the tabernacle has a very special significance. It contains the elements, which represent the very presence of the body and blood of Christ in the church. When later she went out from Trent with her companions, she would look lovingly at the churches she passed on the way. There, in each church, were the tabernacles where he dwelt. 'Every church we glimpsed from the window of the train meant "home" for the soul.' Thus the Eucharist meant Christ in the world, not just a formal doctrine, but the living body of Christ present. And every church declared this to the world. His presence in so many churches made the world a beautiful place. Her own words were: 'The world was not then so ugly; Jesus Himself in the Eucharist made a limitless cloister of it and offered food for that hunger for the divine which can arise in anyone.'

Chiara Lubich, October 1976

Each year, the movement chooses a theme and it was 'The Eucharist' in 1977. In preparation for the study of the theme throughout the movement, Chiara always consults with various leading figures in the different branches. She then studies carefully, both the Bible and the Church Fathers, and gives a series of talks which are then printed and circulated throughout the world. Nowadays there are also videos recorded of her talks. In 1976, she spoke on 'The Eucharist' – four talks. The text was printed and published in 1977 by *Città Nuova*.[1] Seeing with the eyes of faith, rendered clearer by love, she presented the mystery of the Eucharist under four headings:

1.   Treasures selected from the Bible and the Church Fathers;
2.   The celebration of the Eucharist in the life of the Church;
3.   The Eucharist as the unity with Christ and with each other;
4.   The Eucharist among men.

The movement has specialised in the Church Fathers. In England, for example, few publishing houses still reproduce so many texts, studies and translations of the Greek and Latin early Fathers as does New City. In this book of the four talks on the Eucharist, Chiara builds up quotations into a kind of cathedral structure. It is beautifully composed and the quotations gain by their juxtaposition to each other. It is not an argument, but a

presentation of a consistent framework for understanding
the Eucharist. It is a work of love, presented modestly,
because one can say only a little about this great mystery.
Yet it must be spoken and she takes courage from a 'Word
of Life' in Paul's Letter to the Galatians 2:20: 'It is no
longer I who live, but Christ who lives in me.' Her careful
reading of the Fathers and also of that unique document
of the early Church, the *Didache* (probably AD 100) leads
her to list the fundamental conditions for the receiving of
the Eucharist. They are in no way judgemental and quite
extraordinarily acceptable to non-Catholics. They take us
to the heart of what makes the Eucharist meaningful to
the believer of whatever tradition. Though they are not
original, they throw light upon the spirituality of Chiara
herself and of the movement:

> The fundamental conditions are: to believe in the
> teaching of Christ; to be baptized; particularly to
> have faith in that which is the Eucharist; to live
> according to the instructions of Christ; to repent
> and to confess one's sins in order to approach the
> Eucharist with a pure heart; to be reconciled with
> the brethren and in the bonds of peace; to be at
> one with the Church and with the bishop; to desire
> that union with Christ and the brethren which the
> Eucharist realises.

The Parish

Until that choice of 'The Eucharist' as the theme for
1977, Chiara had not written much on the subject.
The Eucharist was so much part of her life that it
needed no special study. She simply lived it, receiving
the body of Christ as the gracious gift of the Church.
She was, and remains, a devout Catholic for whom
the Eucharist is nourishment to her soul. Those who
followed her were at first mostly Catholic and the
teaching of the Church was enough for them. They
distinguished themselves by their frequent communion.

This became particularly evident in the New Parish Movement. There were many parishes badly in need of new life. So many were desperately trying to become relevant, dwindling in a non-religious atmosphere. They were all too often merely on the defensive against secular attacks. In many Italian parishes, in the early years of the movement, priests complained that the pressure of economic conditions, of social and political problems had left contemporary man unable to find God. The churches, they said, were simply serving a minority of people and performing merely routine and bureaucratic functions. They were, in other words, dispirited. When a focolare moved into the parish, their freshness and their devotion brought a new hope to many a priest. The first change they made was to help people modify their concept of the parish and sometimes helping the priest to do the same.

For the focolarini, the church was not simply a place in which to live religion, it was a presence. Christ had taken up his dwelling there in order to be among the people. The Eucharist proclaimed this visually, but it was in any case, the only way to think of a church or parish – where Christ dwells with those who come together in his name. 'Christ comes alive in our midst,' they would say, 'to help us, to sustain us in our difficulties and to enlighten us amidst our problems, to become our companion, to reunite us day by day.' The presence of the tabernacle could remind us all of this. Christ in our midst was seen in the context of the Trinity, the model of our unity. When a congregation is united in a parish – loving one another as the Son loves the Father – then even the simple things like walking, working, resting, become ways of living the entire day with Jesus present. This way of life helps many to understand the Eucharist and there are stories told by priests of how the Focolare have done more than all their teaching had to show the importance of communion. One told of a theological student who said:

For some time I have asked myself if it is true that Jesus is still alive. Then I met a community living

united in the name of Jesus and I said to myself, 'He
is truly present.' Now I understand the Eucharist,
the Church, the Sacaments and also authority in
an entirely different way. I can also say that when
a community accepts Jesus, he dwells there and the
parishoners become his members, his body. I have
found the Church.'

That theological student had grasped the essence of
'Jesus in the midst' in the Focolare sense. I have heard
much the same reactions from priests in Palermo and
in Noto, those described in the chapter on Sicily. But
it does not have to be a Catholic church. Anglican,
Lutheran and Reformed can all see the effect of a group
of Focolarini in their midst. The most noticeable effect
these people living the Ideal have upon a local church
is often to give new meaning to old traditional practices,
which had become routine. New life is what comes
into a congregation with such commitment to unity
and love of God. In particular the Eucharist comes
alive and vital for everyday living, whether it be the
Mass, the Eucharist, the Holy Communion, the Lord's
Supper or the Breaking of Bread. All traditions can
respond to an injection of new life. This is not done
by any personal or original innovations or reforms, but
by members acquiring a new understanding, through a
new attitude to the presence of Christ.

What this means, in effect, is that the old disputes
about the 'real presence' are put into the background,
while each tradition follows its own way of adoring the
Lord's presence. It is not explanations that are needed,
but the experience of being in the presence of the Lord. In
this way the experience is deeper and the worship more
profound. It is an experiential understanding of the real
presence of Christ in the Eucharist.

Even in the Reformed churches where, despite many
efforts and in contradiction to the teaching of Calvin
himself, the Communion Service has taken second place
to preaching, the Focolare have given prominence to the

practice of making the eucharistic mystery the centre of one's whole life. Of course, this has been aided by the liturgical movements in all of the Reformed churches and is not due entirely to the Focolare Movement. But the fact that we have seen a liturgical movement in these churches makes them more responsive to what the Focolare have to offer.

The renewal was also necessary in the Catholic churches, where Mass is often a dry duty rather than a living experience. Reported comments, from many parts of the world, say that when a focolare group has come to town, or at least to the parish, the worship of the church there has been revitalised by their devotion. Such remarks as, 'in coming to Mass in your church I have found God', 'You are a real community', 'Your Mass gives me strength for the entire week', show the effect of the New Parish Movement in many local churches. Its aim is 'to establish living communities made up of Christians who are bound together by mutual love and thus able to generate the presence of Christ in their midst'. This leads to a revitalising of the worship of the parish and a rediscovery of the mystery of the Eucharist.

The Difficulties of Language

The choice of the Eucharist as the theme for 1977 presented the most formidable problems for those attracted to the movement from Protestant churches. A similar problem came the following year when 'the Hierarchy' was chosen as the theme, but fortunately we do not have to deal with that here! Chiara is never obscure. She speaks directly and she speaks out of a rich tradition of Catholic spirituality. In her presentation in those four talks she was as usual, uncompromising and clear. Many a Protestant found her language difficult, but sensed a kinship in her spiritual discernment, as I did. It made us penetrate into the language to discover what it was she was saying to us. With the authority of the teaching of the Catholic Church supported by John 6:53–54: 'Unless

you eat the flesh of the Son of man and drink his blood,
you have no life in you; he who eats my flesh and drinks
my blood has eternal life' (John 6:53), she declares that
Christ is there in the broken bread. When we eat that
bread we eat his flesh and he becomes part of us, or rather
we become part of him. Unlike ordinary food we do not
change it into ourselves, but it changes us. We become
like Christ and he 'will raise us up on the last day'. The
Eucharist, constantly and faithfully received means that
Christ is formed in us.

That is not easy for a Protestant to accept, but try
to penetrate beneath the language which in such cases
is always inadequate. Lovers will often complain that
they have not language enough to express their love.
How much truer this is when we seek to explain the
mystery of the Eucharist. We all declare that Christ is
present – the Real presence – but our language falters
as we explain.

Chiara goes further and takes that great poem in Paul's
Letter to the Romans in chapter 8 verses 18–23, and
gives a new interpretation to the sentence, 'The creation
waits with eager longing for the revealing of the sons of
God'. It is true that that passage opens up a vision of
a new heaven and a new earth linked to our redemption.
But Chiara links it with the Eucharist and suggests
that the saints who have died and been buried are
co-operating with God in the renewal of the earth. Thus
the bodies of the faithful who have been buried, because
they are formed by Christ, put Christ into the earth
and renew it. Such mystical language is alien to most
Protestants and can revive all the old, bitter controversies
about transubstantiation. Chiara does not engage in such
controversies. We have to hear her differently. This is
not John of Gaunt trying to dissuade John Wycliffe
from publishing his tract against transubstantiation. It
is Chiara giving a broad and mystical interpretation to
the effect of the Eucharist on those who receive it in
faith. We are asked to listen to this as spiritual language,
having nothing to do with chemistry and physics. It is not

a chemical analysis of the host, but an affirmation of the real presence. What is received in the Eucharist is Christ. The death of a saint, of all the generations of saints, does help God to renew the earth.

Chiara, however, has used something much stronger than a figure of speech. She has spoken spiritual language and just as she always sees the outlines of the spiritual in the physical, she here discerns the outlines of the physical in the spiritual. Teilhard de Chardin has much the same attitude to the physical, as in his prayer concerning death:

> When I feel I am losing hold of myself and am absolutely passive within the hands of the great unknown forces that have formed me; in all these dark moments, O God, grant that I may understand that it is you who are painfully parting the fibres of my being in order to penetrate the very marrow of my substance and bear me away within yourself.

Chiara's views on the Eucharist must be received and taken into one's system, not discussed in terms of the old, arid eucharistic debates that have so long divided the Church. As we listen, Chiara's great charisma of unity becomes clear.

Intercommunion

One of the constant questions asked by all who seek unity is that of intercommunion. There can be no complete unity in the Church until we share the Lord's Table, receiving from each other the precious gift of the bread and the wine. Only a generation ago, Anglicans and Free Church members sorrowed that the Table was divided. Partly that sorrow has been removed. But with the Catholics we still have no intercommunion. The sorrow remains and the difficulty lies in the two different views of the way in which God will unite his scattered Church. The common Table may be viewed either as the goal to which we move, the celebration of unity achieved, or

the means by which we come together. The Focolare
Movement, rooted in the Catholic Church understands
the path to unity primarily in the former way and follows
the teaching of the Church. Intercommunion cannot be,
either in theory or practice, so long as the Church is
divided. It is a great sorrow to members of the movement
that they cannot receive the Eucharist together, given
the strong bond of spiritual unity they experience with
Jesus in the midst. The spiritual key that unlocks the
door dividing us is the proper love of the cross, the love
of Jesus Forsaken, seen under the aspect of not being able
to participate in the Eucharist together.

Joan Back, in a book to which I shall refer in detail
in the next chapter, unravels the problem, but does
not remove the sorrow: 'After years of looking at the
spirituality of different traditions, two principles of great
ecumenical importance have been established.'

In plain language, the first of these principles is that
Catholic and Protestant may be together at the eucharistic
celebration in whichever form and because Jesus is in the
midst as he promised, there is a strong sense of spiritual
communion – issuing from the Eucharist.

The second is that when we are together in such a way
that we are one despite the division, then, in loving and
embracing Jesus Forsaken, we receive the same gifts of
the Holy Spirit, experiencing this in the soul even though
we do not receive. Behind that second principle lies the
practice of many focolarini in union with their friends of
another tradition: to receive for them.

This is spiritual intercommunion, an anticipation of the
day when in God's own way the Church will be one.

When Joan Back wrote her thesis on 'The Contribution
of the Focolare Movement to the Ecumenical *Koinonia*
(Communion)', she described the movement as 'a spirituality of our time in the service of unity': 'In the *koinonia*,
a way is created for spiritual communion with Jesus in
the midst, which is an anticipation of participation in the
same Eucharist, given that the Eucharist expresses the
fulness of the unity of the Church'.

Chiara, in her own style, says much the same: 'To-morrow all will be reunited. By what means will this come about? First, by means of reciprocal love which establishes Jesus in the midst of us. Placing Jesus in the midst of us finds its completion in its highest point which is the Eucharist.'

Joan Back lists the main tenets of the spirituality of the movement, ranging from the earliest compelling concept which, amidst the hatred and destruction of the Second World War, affirmed that God is love, to the will of God, Jesus in the neighbour, the new commandment, unity, Jesus in the midst, Jesus Forsaken, the Word of Life, the Eucharist, Mary, the Church, the Holy Spirit. Twelve points to be constantly remembered in assessing the spirituality of this movement. Of the Eucharist, Joan Back writes:

The Eucharist is considered as a pivotal point of the spirituality; its effect, as the Fathers of the Church said, is the transformation of man into God: a divination in the sense that the Christian is changed into the Christ he receives. From the beginning, members of the movement have desired spontaneously to receive Jesus in the Eucharist daily. Chiara has commented that this is one of the principal reasons why the unity created within the Movement has been so strong. To this extent, the Eucharist is not only a sign of unity achieved, but also a means whereby the sacrament becomes the cause: 'Jesus before he prayed to the Father that "all may be one; even as thou, Father, art in me, and I in thee . . ."' (John 17:21), instituted the sacrament which made this possible in all its fulness.[2]

The Heavenly Mariapolis

When a focolarino or focolarina dies, it is customary to say that he or she has gone to the heavenly Mariapolis. As in life, the focolarini find refreshment each year in

a Mariapolis where they live the Ideal with others and
demonstrate to those who are not of their number what it
means to love one another in loving God and to experience
Jesus in the midst. What is more natural then than to talk
of heaven as an everlasting Mariapolis . . .

In the last weeks of life, the Eucharist becomes of
growing significance for many. I can illustrate this best by
recalling the death of Igino Giordani, whom I knew well.

While I was writing his biography, he was seriously
ill and passed over to the heavenly Mariapolis. I was
not there when he died nor at his celebration funeral.
I learnt of his last weeks later from one of his closest
friends, a member of his focolare, Antonio Petrilli.

Igino, despite his very distinguished career as a politician and author, his great piety and saintliness, his role
as co-founder of the Focolare Movement, insisted upon
being treated as an ordinary focolarino. But he inspired
such love and devotion that this was almost impossible.

When he became very ill and it was obvious that he
would not live for more than a few weeks, those members
of his focolare who lived with him in Rocca di Papa served
him like priests at an altar. The many things that have
to be done for a man in the last days of weakness were,
as Antonio said 'like an act of service and love to Christ
crucified'. This reached its climax when they celebrated
Mass in his room: 'It seemed as though the supernatural
atmospherre reached its peak at that moment.' When
he was asked at what time he wished to receive Jesus
in the Eucharist, he answered like a hungry schoolboy,
'Right now'. 'How lucky I am,' he told those serving
him, 'being able to receive communion here every day.'
However weak and weary he was, the Eucharist came as
refreshment and life. His last 'sermon' on 30th January
1980 was very brief:

Christ unites us to himself through the Eucharist
which is Love, and through suffering which is
divinized love. Thus the commandment of the Last
Supper keeps being transmitted and lived. Christ

redeemed us with suffering and continues to redeem
us through suffering and love.

As the end drew near, Igino's last thoughts were expressed in words he repeated often: 'He who sees his
brother sees the Lord'. This love for Jesus in his neighbour
was so much part of him, that he continued giving of
himself to others. Those who were there to help him,
told me that they ended up being helped by him. Antonio
expressed it most clearly: 'His love for Christ was so
deeply rooted that those around him were unaware of his
daily suffering as he offered up his painful illness to God.
This love seemed to absorb all suffering and transformed
it into itself.'

One final quote from the dying Igino himself: 'We have
never been so much one with Jesus as we are now when,
crucified with him, we can give him the joy of our living
participation.'

CHAPTER EIGHT
POINTS OF CONTACT

On 24th May 1961, Chiara founded an ecumenical secretariat, called *Centro 'Uno'*, with the first married focolarino as its director: Igino Giordani. The role of Giordani in the movement is of such importance that he is often referred to as its co-founder. He directed the ecumenical secretariat until his death in 1980. It was situated in Rome and his work was carried on after his death by Gabriella Fallacara, who now directs it from a focolare in Grottaferrata. On the staff of *Centro 'Uno'* is a focolarina from Liverpool called Joan Patricia Back. She graduated in English Literature from the University of Liverpool, has been at *Centro 'Uno'* since 1975 and has studied theology in Rome. Her thesis which she wrote for her Doctorate of Theology at the Lateran Pontifical University, is entitled, *Il contributo del Movimento dei Focolari alla Koinonia Ecumenica*, (The contribution of the Focolare Movement to the Ecumenical Koinonia, or Communion). Its sub-title is 'A Spirituality for our time at the service of unity'.

Her thesis is that the aim of all the dialogue between churches and religious communities to re-establish full communion within the Church has its roots in the discovery of the ecclesiology of 'communion'. She uses the Greek and New Testament word *'koinonia'*. It is most simply understood in the words of Paul to the Corinthians, when he is describing the Church as a healthy, living body with all its members working:

But God has harmonised the whole body by giving

importance of function to the parts which lack apparent importance, that the body should work together as a whole with all the members in sympathetic relationship with one another. So it happens that if one member suffers all the other members suffer with it, and if one member is honoured all the members share a common joy. (1 Cor. 12:24–26, J.B. Phillips)

That is 'koinonia'. And for Joan Back, it is the key word for the ecumenical movement today. Within its setting she finds that there are several elements in Focolare spirituality which find an echo in other traditions. With the Anglicans there is a special bond in the desire for unity; with the Orthodox, it is the central role of love in a mystical theology; with the Lutherans, it is the Word of God, illustrated in the Focolare spirituality by the central role in the daily life of its members of the 'Word of Life'; with the Reformed Churches, the point of contact is the presence of Jesus in the midst, the recognition that Jesus is specially present when the faithful gather together.

Lutherans and Anglicans

The role of Chiara in mediating this spiritı ality, which the movement sees as God's gift to her, her charisma, is crucial. She has herself made the contacts which were necessary with various branches of the Christian Church.

Having initiated the ecumenical work of the movement in 1960, she lost no time in making personal contacts with other traditions.

In 1961, she went to Darmstadt in Germany to meet Lutheran deaconesses and ministers. In the same year she met Canon Bernard Pawley, an Anglican observer at the Second Vatican Council and there began a fruitful exchange between Anglicans and Catholics in the movement. It was following these two meetings that she saw the importance of starting up Centro 'Uno'. Then, on her fifth visit to Germany she addressed a mixed audience of Protestants and Catholics at the summer Mariapolis at Violau. It was later in October of that year that she

entertained in Rome the first group of Protestant friends
of the movement.

In 1962, Chiara met the Lutheran Bishop of Bavaria,
Dr. Hermann Dietzfelbinger and during Holy Week in
Alexandersbad, she spoke to a meeting of 150 Lutherans.
At Pentecost, *Centro 'Uno'* arranged a conference of
Catholics and Lutherans from Germany. This led in
October, 1963 to a meeting at Ottmaring, near Augsburg,
with the Lutheran 'Brotherhood of the Common Life'. In
the same year, the first focolare was opened in England
at Liverpool.

The contact with the 'Brotherhood of the Common Life'
was most fruitful and it had the blessing of the Lutheran
Bishop of Bavaria. With the full agreement of the Catholic
and Lutheran hierarchies, it was agreed to set up an
ecumenical centre at Ottmaring jointly with the 'Brotherhood of the Common Life' and the 'Focolare Movement'.

Ottmaring

As relations with the Lutherans developed, a centre at
Ottmaring was opened in 1968. It was a village in which
focolarini priests and laity lived together side by side with
an existing community and using two parish churches –
Catholic and Lutheran. The Focolare buildings grew over
the years and demonstrated the unity of Catholics and
Lutheran 'Brethren of the Common Life'. This ecumenical
centre of life *(Oekumanisches Lebenszentrum)* celebrated
its 20th anniversary in November, 1988. Ottmaring is near
to Friedberg, a beautiful Bavarian town under the shadow
of Augsburg, once the financial centre of Europe. Earlier
in the year Chiara had been honoured with the Augsburg
Peace Award, commemorating the Peace of Augsburg in
1555 when Catholics and Protestants agreed to recognise
each other (*'Cuius regio, eius religio'*).

The centre at Ottmaring, as I saw it at that time,
was very extensive with a thriving community of 120,
some living in houses in the village nearby and others
in the Community Centre. They are still equally divided

between Catholics and Lutherans. The Catholic Parish Church is in the village itself, the Lutheran in the next village. Both are strongly supported by the community. In the centre there is also united worship and meditation. There is, of course, as in all focolare activity, sharing, unity and always 'Jesus in the midst'. The Focolare characteristic of hospitality is most evident and there are guest rooms and guest houses. Pictures of Chiara and Igino Giordani can be seen, but there is also an excellent taste in artistic decor and the choice of paintings. The whole centre strikes one as tastefully designed and extremely pleasant to be in. From it relations between Catholics and Lutherans are developed successfully. On the evening of the celebration of the 20th anniversary, which was held in the town hall of Friedberg, 1,200 were present and Chiara's place in the hearts of all was unmistakably evident. Visitors from outside may find this appreciation of Chiara a little excessive but it is by no means sought by her. It comes from gratitude and love for all that her spiritual gift from God has brought to the movement. The celebration was a typically Focolare event, with the now famous music groups called 'Gen Verde' and 'Gen Rosso'. But it was also a very public event with speakers from church and state pointing out the contribution which the centre at Ottmaring had made to the whole community in that part of Bavaria.

The Church of England

Although the first focolare was opened in England as early as 1963, Chiara's main impact on the Church of England came when she was awarded the Templeton Prize in 1977 for 'progress in religion'. She had met two archbishops before – Michael Ramsey and Geoffrey Fisher in retirement. This time she met Donald Coggan who was more of a biblical evangelical than the other two. He still retains a great appreciation of her work. Many had expected that, because of the Catholic predominance in the movement, it would appeal to the

Anglo-Catholic element in the Church of England rather
than the evangelical wing. This was true at first, but
there had long been a search for a more meditative
emphasis among Protestants and evangelicals, to which
the Focolare Movement offered much. Donald Coggan
saw this, although he was less at home with some
elements of the movement than Michael Ramsey had
been. Chiara was in England again in 1981 for a very
important meeting with Archbishop Robert Runcie, who
of all the archbishops understood her vision best and
appreciated her work most. He awarded her the 'Order of
Saint Augustine of Canterbury' for her ecumenical work
among Anglicans, and appointed Bishop John Dennis as
episcopal guardian of the Anglicans of the movement.
A few days later she opened an Ecumenical School
for members of the movement in England. As I write,
arrangements are in hand for Chiara to meet the present
Archbishop, George Carey, who has also agreed to write
the preface to this book.

1965 was a good year for relations with the Church of
England. In June, a group of Anglicans participated in an
ecumenical rally of the Focolare Movement. At that time,
they met Cardinal Bea, then head of the 'Secretariat
for Promoting Christian Unity' at the Vatican. He saw
the possibilities of Catholic/Anglican relations within the
Focolare Movement and said so. In November, Chiara
spoke in the Anglican Cathedral in Liverpool.

In January, 1967 she was invited to Canterbury to
address a meeting organised by Canon Bernard Pawley
during the Week of Prayer for Christian Unity.

There is no doubt that those who she met on these various occasions were persuaded that the Focolare Movement had something special to offer to the Church of
England.

The Greek Orthodox Church

The closest bond that Chiara made with any 'church'
other than her own was with the Greek Orthodox Church.

This was due in no small measure to her meetings with the Ecumenical Patriarch Athenagoras. The first of these meetings was in June, 1967, but there were many others held over the next few months. The Patriarch gave her more than a sympathetic hearing. He found her aspirations towards unity almost identical with his own. 'You are my daughter,' he said. 'You have two fathers: a great one in Rome, Paul VI (for whom the Patriarch had a very high regard, speaking of him as 'a second St. Paul'!) and another, an old one, in me, here.'

In her interviews with Franca Zambonini, Chiara showed how greatly she appreciated the Patriarch, both because of his spirituality, which linked him very closely with Pope Paul VI, but also his hospitality.

'I learnt,' she said, 'about the quality of charity which must always take priority over any conversation we might be planning. We never got down to talking before he had offered and I had accepted some gesture of hospitality such as a coffee. He wanted to pay for the hotel I stayed in, because he wanted me to be his guest. At the *Fanar* where we would meet, there was always a room prepared with the greatest attention for me to dine in. Even on the days when the Orthodox were fasting and abstaining, he did not want to inconvenience me in any way and so for me there was . . . caviar.'

What is striking about that memory of the Patriarch's hospitality is that it describes perfectly the kind of hospitality which I have always experienced with the Focolare, in London and in Rome, in East Berlin and in Melbourne, in Trent and in Stuttgart. The 'gesture of hospitality' is the mark of the Focolare Movement wherever one meets it and it is the same to whomsoever it is offered.

Athenagoras taught Chiara a great deal and her response to his spirituality influenced the whole movement. In particular, she noted how he loved all peoples – finding the good in the worst of them. Again a Focolare characteristic.

'During his long life,' she said, 'he had got to know many people and knew how to see goodness everywhere. I do not know how he did it, but I am sure that he had a special gift in this regard.'

She might have been describing herself, but she added: 'From him I learnt to love all nations, to find the good in them all.'

Chiara played a significant role as a go-between, enabling Pope Paul VI and the Patriarch to converse informally. She had a close relationship with Pope Paul VI and would convey to him the sentiments of Athenagoras, particularly of his longing to re-establish full communion with the Roman Church. The growing relationship between these two leaders of great Churches which had been divided for a thousand years was helped by Chiara. When Athenagoras died, Paul VI remarked, 'A saint has died'.

Chiara continued her efforts with his successor, Dimitrios I, who also showed great interest in the movement.

Contacts with Other Churches

Though the Focolare Movement is overwhelmingly Catholic, its spirituality has appealed to Christians of all denominations. Not in large numbers, nor always to the extent of total commitment to the movement. But by the end of 1987, which is the latest date for which I have figures, there were more than 30,000 living the spirituality of the movement, while adhering loyally to a tradition other than that of the Roman Catholic Church. More than 200 different denominations and Christian communities are included in those figures. The largest group is from the Lutherans, whose relationship with the movement is institutionalised in the community at Ottmaring. There were more than 13,000 who owed allegiance to the Evangelical Lutheran Church; more than 3,000 came from the Reformed Churches; but next to the Lutherans, it is the Anglicans who have found most help in the movement. There were at that time about 8,000 Anglicans living the Focolare spirituality. Despite the strong links with the Patriarch Athenagoras, the Orthodox Churches have contributed no more than 1,600. For the rest, only three denominations number more than 500 – Baptists, Methodists and Presbyterians.

These figures may have changed considerably since the end of 1987, but I think the pattern has remained the same.

A section of the Lutheran Church, particularly communities such as the 'Brotherhood of the Common Life', found an immediate rapport with the movement. Michael Ramsey, the first Archbishop of Canterbury to come into contact with Chiara, saw at once its appeal to certain spiritual movements within the Anglican Communion. When he greeted Chiara, he said that he immediately 'recognised the hand of God in this movement' and encouraged her to 'build a spiritual communion with them so that hearts might be warmed by this spirit'. The Reformed Churches, among whom are the Baptists and the Presbyterians, recognised in the return to the spirituality of the New Testament, something akin to their 'constant reformation', and the Methodists have felt sympathy with the search for holiness. Despite much that appeals, there are nonetheless centuries of conflict to overcome, in meeting a movement so obviously grounded in the spirituality of the Catholic Church. A closer acquaintance shows that the Catholic Church of the Focolare Movement is that of the Early Fathers in whom Chiara and other Focolare writers base much of their theological reasoning. This inevitably appeals to the Orthodox Church. It also helps Protestants to get behind the Reformation to a time before the great divide. In fact, the Greek Fathers and the early Latins who play such a large part in the Focolare literature are before Constantine. It is, perhaps the pre-Constantine Catholic Church that we recognise in the Focolare Movement. There we all have common ground. The unity lies in our origin. Today we are divided and the loyalty which the Focolare Movement encourages in all traditions makes

it possible for us to live in this unity, without denying
our history.

Other Religions

When Chiara received the Templeton Prize for 'Progress in Religion' in 1977, she met a group of Asians
and asked herself about the relationship between the
Focolare Movement and other religions. Here she trod
on controversial ground, but with her usual honesty
and forthrightness. She was never without courage. The
question of other religions remained until she met the full
attraction of Buddhism.

In her book, *Incontri con l'Oriente* (1987), Chiara
describes her experiences with the great religious traditions of Asia. In particular she comments upon her
personal relationship with the Japanese Buddhist leader,
Nikkyo Niwano. In 1979 he also received the Templeton
Prize and on his way to London to receive it he stopped
in Rome. He asked if he could meet Chiara, a former
prize winner, but he had other matters on his mind to
discuss with her. Some young people from the organisation he founded – *Rissho-Kosei-kai* – had met focolarini in
Japan, in the USA and in Rome. He was anxious to know
what had attracted his young people to this Christian
movement. Chiara was looking for some sign to follow
up her initial insight that the movement should make
contact with believers of other religions. The young people
of both movements had found something in common.
Nikkyo Niwano was prepared to believe that, because
of an experience he had had in 1964, during the second
Vatican Council, when he met Pope Paul VI. When Chiara
met Nikkyo, he described the effect of that earlier meeting
with the Pope: 'He spoke of that meeting with awe,'
Chiara said, 'because it was then he had understood that
he had to dedicate his whole life to a greater understanding between the religions of the East and the West.'

After this meeting he helped to found the World Conference for Religion and Peace, and became its Honorary

President. The meeting with Chiara in Rome in 1979, convinced both of them that the two movements could work together. He invited Chiara to Tokyo to describe her spiritual experiences to the leaders of his organisation. In 1981, she went to Tokyo and spoke, not only to the leaders, but to a vast assembly of the young people of this Buddhist movement. In the Sacred Hall in Tokyo, 10,000 Japanese listened to Chiara tell the story of her spiritual pilgrimage, while ten video monitors relayed the event to the crowded foyer and corridors outside. That event on 28th December 1981, was one of the greatest witnesses to young Buddhists. Jesus Christ was glorified. Chiara does not change her message to suit her audience. She told of her Christian experience of 'Jesus in the midst', of 'Jesus Forsaken', of her love for Mary the mother of Jesus and of the Ideal which she and more than a million others live throughout the world.

Chiara's own comment about her meetings with Nikkyo Niwano in Tokyo shows her loyalty to her faith and clears her of all charges of syncretism:

> I remember feeling so free with him and being able to speak openly of my Christian faith; I think we spoke of little else other than of Jesus. The truth is that an opening had been made for me because of the witness of the Gospel life seen in the movement's communities which had so deeply impressed the youth of the *Rissho-Kosei-kai* and Nikkyo Niwano himself.

It was during these conversations that she saw a dialogue with Buddhists to be possible and that it might be a form of 'evangelism'. She was convinced that the Holy Spirit was preparing them for this dialogue by teaching them that above all they must love, make themselves one with the other person, and transform suffering into love and joy. With this preparation she could see good in much of the Buddhist teaching, which she felt must prepare the way for 'the proclamation of Christ and of Christ crucified, of the One who went to the cross in order to conquer suffering and death'.

Buddhists, who sought by their four noble truths to extinguish suffering, would surely understand that. But Buddhists, she saw, have to experience Christ as they touch him in individual Christians. This can only happen if we have in us something of Christ's own love, that love which makes us ready to give our lives for others.

Her joy came in 1985 when she was once again invited to Tokyo to the celebration of Nikkyo's eightieth birthday. Once again in the great Sacred Hall in Tokyo, she saw the vast crowds of young people of the *Rissho-Kosei-kai* listening to the founder. He said, in the course of his talk that afternoon to the Buddhist youth, that 'should their consciences urge them to become Christians, they should do so'.

The Poverty of Brazil

On 12th May 1991, Chiara arrived in Brazil. It was her second visit. She had conceived the idea of implanting the Focolare Movement in Brazil as early as 1959. One of her earliest companions, Ginetta, left for Brazil in November 1959, with Marco, Volo and others. As she bade them fare-well, Chiara said, 'I am entrusting you with a crucifix, not of wood, but a living Crucified One, Jesus Forsaken.' She visited them first in 1966. Now in 1991 it was a whole generation later, and she came to a very different Brazil. She made her usual triumphal tour of the Focolare communities, but this time she did so by remaining in Aracoeli, which is a Brazilian form of Loppiano. They came to her or sent messages and gifts. She was showered with gifts of love, but she also brought her own. From the central fund of the movement she brought money to help the Focolare of Brazil do their work of loving the poor. She outlined how this might be done. The poor in Brazil, as elsewhere, lack work, adequate housing, adequate food, but most of all a sense that anyone cares for them. The Focolare Movement must show it cares, she said. This is done personally, but social problems have to be tackled and Chiara saw a way. The money could be used to build small factories in the poorest areas and thus to stimulate the sharing of profits and development in favour of the poor. The profits from such factories would go into the development of the industry and some of it to relieve the immediate hardship of those who could not be employed. The awful problem of poverty and deprivation in Brazil has beaten some of the cleverest minds. Chiara, in her matter of fact way, began small. If you can't do all, then do something. The small factories would engender communities and in these communities love could be shown. The squadrons of love were in action.

Brazil is only one example of the way in which the Focolare Movement has moved into the social and political sphere in many parts of the world without losing the Ideal.

After Chiara had visited some of the small centres with their practical work, she came to Sao Paulo and like every other visitor there she marvelled at the city of skyscrapers. In her diary that day she wrote:

At last I have visited the men's focolare: the focolarini who live there were waiting for me at the entrance. It's a spacious, modern building, furnished with simplicity, but with a harmonious touch which makes it welcoming. In a comfortable sitting room I had a meeting with the 5 focolarini responsible for the zones of Brazil: it was a happy, festive, informal meeting. Among other things we spoke of the 'miraculous' growth of the city of Sao Paulo: in 1900 it was a little village. Nowadays it is nothing short of a forest of skyscrapers. Capital in the hands of a few people and exploitation of others is very powerful. But why – we asked ourselves – can this power not be geared towards solving the pressing problems of Brazil? Because brotherly love is lacking, and competition and egoism predominate. When Jesus is absent, the world is such a caricature. We must grow until good goes ahead of its own accord. There is hope and – I would say – certainty of this. You can see it above all in the faces of the focolarini whom I met this evening in their houses.

It was characteristic of Chiara that, when she was about to leave Brazil, she wrote in her diary that that very morning at the Eucharist, she had heard two 'Words of Life' which confirmed what she had started in Brazil: 'Do not think of yourselves more highly than you ought' (Romans 12:3). 'The mighty One has done great things for me' (Luke 1:49, from Magnificat).

She commented that while we make little things, they are rendered great by God working in us.

Stuttgart

Many examples could be described of these little things that have been transformed by God into great endeavours. When I have been to vast gatherings of the Focolare Movement, whether to hear and see the performances of Gen Verde (an international group of focolarine, singing, dancing, miming the message of unity), or to international theme conferences in the Sports Palace in Rome, or to witness the international spread into Africa, Asia and Latin America, I have marvelled at the great things God has done. But the mighty oak comes from the acorn and the seed of this success lies in the little things attempted by people who do not think more highly of themselves than they ought.

As I came to the end of writing this book, I visited a focolare in Stuttgart, which is predominately a Protestant town in Germany. It was the one focolare in the town, just four young women. They offered their usual hospitality to me and brought two Gen and a Focolare priest to spend an evening talking about what we believed and how it influenced our lives. It was a beautiful evening, demonstrating everything I knew about the Focolare Movement. But it was no great thing – it was a beautiful little thing, such as God makes great.

EPILOGUE

To cover adequately the spirituality of the Focolare Movement would require more than one small book. Fortunately, those who are interested will find many books published by New City, the English publishing firm of the Movement. Or perhaps, better still, will meet a focolare. At the end of this book I have given some addresses for contacts.

In this epilogue, I want to address myself to my fellow Protestants on the broad issues of *koinonia* (usually translated, 'communion' which is a word we often use for Eucharist).

It is not possible to be with anyone from this movement without recognising that they are part of the body of Christ. They have perhaps been given the special task of unifying the body. It has arisen from a part of the Church with which we have had many disagreements in the past. The Focolare Movement does not come to make us all into Roman Catholics. It comes to us as a gift from God and we should allow that gift to penetrate our various traditions.

In my own experience of many years working in the ecumenical movement, with the World Council of Churches, with the United Bible Societies and in the field of broadcasting, I have seen God at work, preparing us for some kind of unity. The Focolare Movement does not have negotiations between traditions, like some international peace treaties. It looks both backwards and forwards. First, back to that early unity, which belonged to the Church fresh from the hands of its Master, a unity that

Christ prayed would be sustained (John 17). That was a period before those great divisions, which stand like milestones along the road of our long history. In their time they were precious, because they preserved great truths sometimes neglected by the Church; they corrected abuses and corruption in the Church. But looking back now, they often stand like gravestones, preventing the life of the Spirit resurrecting the unity of the Church. Their total effect today is seen as destructive. Very early, the Church nearly divided – into Jewish and Gentile Christians, the mystical scriptures of Alexandria divided from the historical interpretation of Antioch, the fierce arguments over the divinity of Christ and the relationship of the Son to the Father, the mixed blessing of Constantine, the 'Christian' Emperor, the medieval intolerance of new insights and of mysticism, the great divide of East and West, the Reformation and its own splinters, the evangelical revival of a moribund Church, the challenge of secularism, the Modernist crisis. We are still being divided.

This movement has come to us with the commitment of the early Church, and the pattern of the second century. It has taught us the importance of living the Word of God in the Bible, and revived the spiritual insights of the Early Fathers. It is not the organisation of the Focolare Movement that is its strength, it is its spirituality such as I have tried to describe in this book. God has raised up for us a woman, out of the old unreformed Catholic Church and shown to us, not only the darkness of our divisions, but a way forward in unity and love, which ignores our divisions. If we imitated it separately in our various traditions we should perpetuate our divisions and betray the cause of unity. If we can allow it to penetrate and take the consequences of its effect, we should see a renewal such as God desires. This is not an attempt to bring our shattered remnants together, hoping that in unity there may be strength. It is a call to the whole Church to recognise that it is one and to demonstrate it, in a common spirituality, enriched by all our traditions and inspired by the woman whom God has raised up. In this way perhaps we can persuade the world to believe. It could be the fuel of true evangelisation and give meaning to that hopeful phrase, 'Christians Together'. We would not only study the Bible, but live it; we would share our time and substance with those who needed us; we would look at other Christians with a view to learning from them, rather than teaching them; we would do little things believing that God would make great things out of them; we would see good in all we met, without being blind to the evil; we would seek unity rather than triumph. We would, in fact, be and do all that we know we should be and do! An idealistic picture? Yes. And we would not achieve it, but as we fell there would be those helping us to rise and go on.

When all the marvellous stories of the Focolare Movement are told, the simple conclusion is that these people are trying to live the life that Christ wants us to live. The role of Chiara has been to enable the whole movement to derive benefit from her gift of unity, born in the heart of the Catholic Church. Have we Protestants humility enough to accept what this new and reformed movement in the Catholic Church now offers to us. Can we Christians go in this way, not only together, but hand in hand.

SOME FOCOLARE TERMS –
A GLOSSARY

Every living movement must develop its own vocabulary, either by inventing new terms, as did Teilhard de Chardin, or by taking old ones and giving them new meaning, as did St. Paul. The Focolare have followed St. Paul but their words are Italian, rather than Greek, and as difficult to translate as St. Paul's!

Focolare The word meant 'hearth' or 'fireside'. It is the name of a community of people who live in the same house and are committed to God and to one another. They have normal jobs. There are communities of men and communities of women. The *focolare* is the heart of the movement. Plural, *focolari*.

The word 'Focolare' is also used in a general sense to mean the whole of the movement.

Focolarino A man who lives in a focolare. Plural, *focolarini* – (used also to include the feminine).

Focolarina A woman who lives in a focolare. Plural, *focolarine*.

Ideal The word Ideal is used primarily by the movement to mean God, chosen as the

one aim in life. Secondly, it also means
the spiritual drive and practical commitment necessary for achieving the
choice of God.

Spirituality   This term is used in a general sense
to mean a way of viewing and living
Christianity and, in particular instances,
is used to mean the whole of Christianity
as seen from the viewpoint of the Focolare
Movement.

Charisma   An extraordinary gift from God given to
a person for the good of mankind.

Word of Life   A phrase from Scripture chosen each
month for the Focolare Movement all
over the world. The Word is not only
something to be studied but to be lived
as a command from God. Sometimes a
Word *of Life is given to an individual
as being particularly appropriate to his
or her needs.*

Mariapolis   Literally, city of Mary. This is the name
given to the large annual gathering of
members and friends of the movement.
Permanent Mariapolises are small
towns where young people, families and
priests from different countries live and
work together.

Mariapolis   These are training centres for members
Centres   of the movement.

Volunteers   These are groups of men or women who
take on a voluntary, personal commit-
ment to revitalise the Christian community. They meet weekly in small

groups and they are the backbone for the New Humanity Movement, which will reaffirm in Christian terms the value of human relations and morality in society.

Gen

The new generation of the Focolare Movement and also the name of their magazine.

Gens

The new generation of Seminarians who belong to the Priests' Movement ... 'Gens' is also the name of their magazine.

GenRe

New generation of Religious who are associated with the Focolare Movement. They also have a magazine called 'GenRe'.

International Schools

These are more like the Focolare universities, with courses in theology, philosophy and spirituality of various lengths up to two years. They are at Loppiano (Italy), O'Higgins (Argentina), Aracoeli (Brazil) etc.

The Study Centre

Members of the movement, who have already studied, experience an interdisciplinary understanding of their subject, both spiritually and socially. This can happen effectively in the Study Centre.

Centro Uno

The central secretariat for ecumenical activities of the Focolare Movement.

NOTES

Chapter Two

1 Robertson, Edwin, *Chiara*, Christian Journals (Ireland) Ltd, 1978.

Chapter Five

1 Robertson, Edwin, *The Fire of Love*, New City, London, 1989.

Chapter Six

1 This was only two days before the 'July Plot' of which he was well aware, although he had by then been in prison for 15 months. He was eventually executed for his supposed involvement in that plot which failed.
2 Lyonnet, S, *Il Nuovo Testaments all luce dell 'Antico*, Brescia, 1970, p.92.
3 Congar, E.Y., *Je Crois en l'Esprit Saint*, Vol 1, Paris, 1979, p.79.
4 Lubich, Chiara, *Gesu Abbandonato*, Rome, 1984, pp.113–4. An English translation was published in 1985: *Why Have You Forsaken Me?*, New City, London, 1985, pp.108–9.

Chapter Seven

1 *Città Nuova*, published fortnightly in Rome, is the principal journal of the movement.
2 Lubich, Chiara, *La Spiritualità del Movimento dei Focolari*, Rome, 1984, pp.6–7.

FURTHER READING

Further reading on the life and spirituality of the Focolare Movement

The Fire of Love: a life of Igino Giordani 'Foco', by Edwin Robertson
The story of a war hero, politician, writer and above all man of God who became a co-founder of the Focalare Movement.
New City, London, 1989, ISBN 0 904287 28 9

May They All Be One, by Chiara Lubich
A book that describes the spirituality of the Focolare through the experience of the first group that sprang up under the bombardment of Trent in northern Italy.
New City, London, 1981, ISBN 0 904287 08 4

Why Have You Forsaken Me?
The key to unity by Chiara Lubich. The key to unity and the life of unity described as two sides of the same coin, made up of all the words of the Gospel.
New City, London, 1985, ISBN 0 904287 26 2

From Scripture to Life by Chiara Lubich
Twelve 'words of life' (passages selected from scripture to be lived month by month), with commentaries and accounts of those who have put these words into practice.
New City Press, New York, 1990, 0 911782 83 4

Chiara Lubich: A Life of Unity by Franca Zambonini
Interview by a leading Italian journalist covering previously unpublished facts of the life and spirituality of the foundress of the Focolare Movement.
New City Press, New York: New City, London, 1992,
ISBN 0 904287 45 9

Jesus, His Last Will and Testament by Pasquale Foresi
An outstanding book of practical yet scholarly scriptural meditations.
New City, London, 1987, ISBN 0 904287 27 0

USEFUL ADDRESSES

Mariapolis Centre:
The Focolare Centre for Unity
69 Parkway
Welwyn Garden City
Herts AL8 6HH

Tel. 0707 323 620

Publishing House:
New City
57 Twyford Avenue
London W3 9PZ

Tel. 081 993 6944

Main Centres:
3 Abbeyville Road
London SW4 9LA

34 Earl's Court Square
London SW5 9PQ